THE BACK HOME SERIES

Series Titles

Praise for
Kick Out the Bottom

"Yes, 'kick out the jams' was one generation's provocation, but Mortenson and Kramer inhabited in their youth a heady mixture of punkish aesthetics and neo-hip mysticism. They give us a Detroit that was on the edge of massive re-transformation even as they were themselves on their way to new modes of living. The inner-city education of these two somehow circles around the personality of a suburban quasi-guru. They've never been the same, and neither has Detroit."

—Aldon Lynn Nielsen
George and Barbara Kelly Professor of American Literature
The Pennsylvania State University

"*Kick Out the Bottom* captures the authors' yearning to invent a new world and a new sense of personhood from the bottom up. In Rilkean fashion, *Kick Out the Bottom* explores characters who are willing to change their lives as they endure an archetypal search for meaning via self-estrangement on the way to self-recomposition in Detroit, a post-apocalyptic Parisian bohemia itself experiencing transformations."

—Daniel Morris
Professor of English, Purdue University
editor of *The Cambridge Companion to American Poetry and Politics since 1900*

"*Kick Out the Bottom* is the future of literature, or, to appropriate from the Detroit that the book transcends, we may ask, 'Is there a *Kick Out the Bottom* in your future?' Christopher Kramer and Erik Mortenson ask us why the one-person memoir should be the norm. As two people who find themselves in a new and undefinable Detroit, Kramer and Mortenson share a common language, and, after all, we all borrow from one another. Why must memoir writing be such a lonely task? Perhaps more important, however, as Kramer's and Mortenson's previously lost-to-history mentor advises, 'Why not kick out the bottom and come out the other side?' What comes out is a veritable 'new tense, one that looks backwards but strives to contain a lost moment's impact as it bleeds into the present of the telling.' In many ways, Kramer and Mortenson may have achieved the first post-Walter Benjamin memoir worthy of Benjamin and his theory of temporal intimacies."

—Stephen Paul Miller
Professor of English, St. John's University
author of *Being with a Bullet*

KICK OUT THE BOTTOM

A Shared Account of a Detroit Mystic

Erik Mortenson
Christopher Kramer

Cornerstone Press
Stevens Point, Wisconsin

Cornerstone Press, Stevens Point, Wisconsin 54481
Copyright © 2023 Erik Mortenson & Christopher Kramer
www.uwsp.edu/cornerstone

Printed in the United States of America by
Point Print and Design Studio, Stevens Point, Wisconsin

Library of Congress Control Number: 2023937991
ISBN: 978-1-960329-04-2

Cornerstone Press titles are produced in courses and internships offered by the
Department of English at the University of Wisconsin–Stevens Point.

DIRECTOR & PUBLISHER   EXECUTIVE EDITOR
Dr. Ross K. Tangedal   Jeff Snowbarger

SENIOR EDITORS
Lexie Neeley, Monica Swinick, Kala Buttke

PRESS STAFF
Grace Dahl, Zoie Dinehart, Kirsten Faulkner, Hannah Fenrick, Patrick Fogarty,
Angela Green, Brett Hill, Julia Kaufman, Kenzie Kierstyn, Maddy Mauthe, Lauren
Rudesill, Catriona Scheinost, Maria Scherer, Taylor Schmidt, Arianna Soto, Anthony
Thiel, Cash Van Stiphout, Matt Vancik, Abbi Wasielewski

To All Seekers of the Self

When the student is ready, the teacher will appear. When the student is truly ready, the teacher will disappear.

—Lao Tzu, from the *Tao Te Ching*

Introduction

Detroit has an identity crisis.

For years, the city was synonymous with the automobile. Although Detroit still makes cars, these days it's hard to find anyone who actually works in the factory. Detroit is also known as one of the few predominantly African American cities in America. But now that the uprising in the summer of 1967, that sent whites fleeing to the suburbs, has become more history than reality for a younger generation, derelict buildings are being replaced by lofts and stadiums, and gentrification is well underway. Detroit has long been known as a city for jazz, for funk, for the Motown sound, for electronica, and for garage rock. But its musical heroes, its Temptations, its Carl Craigs, its Eminems and White Stripes now feel like classics, and have all left town. Detroit is looking to rebrand.

What's left is authenticity, and that is fast disappearing. You can see it on the ubiquitous T-shirts that a desire to stand apart from the crowd has spawned. "Detroit Hustles Harder" and "Detroit vs. Everybody" are the best-known examples. This us-against-the-world mentality, this young-kid-just-coming-up attitude plays well, especially to Detroiters. Life in Detroit does feel a bit more difficult than in other urban enclaves. There is true grit. I remember once taking the bus from the Polish section of town, called Hamtramck, to the city's main artery, Woodward Avenue.

It was cold, with a chilling wind carrying flakes of snow across the street. A prostitute crossed in front of me, dressed scantily and obviously cold. Not an abnormal sight, but what arrested attention was that she had put empty potato chip bags on her hands to keep warm. This ingenuity, this perseverance, this "hustle," in all its myriad senses, is Detroit.

This work is an attempt to revive the spirit we encountered in *fin de siècle* Detroit, to capture the possibilities the city offered at the millennium's turn. *Kick Out the Bottom* celebrates a do-it-yourself Detroit that challenged conventions and comfort zones. This is not to say that our experience is any better than that of the Detroiters who came after us. Each experience is unique. Nor can the story of two white men living an "edge" experience in an African American city avoid the contradictions inherent in racially-divided America. For us, Detroit was bohemian; for its long-time residents, it was often a place of struggle. But this work is an attempt to capture an important moment in Detroit's history: a time when meaningful (if fraught) interactions were common; a time before you could eat grilled salmon at Whole Foods or spend hundreds of dollars on a baseball mitt at Shinola; a time when public transit meant engaging fellow passengers on the bus instead of sitting alone in an Uber ride. It was a Detroit that was probably not any more violent than today, but certainly less convenient, and definitely more of the sort of "wasteland" that everyone thought it was before words like "revitalization" or "creative class" took hold. It was a time to run experiments on ourselves, and Detroit was the sort of place where any experiment was permitted.

Kick Out the Bottom, as the name suggests, portrays our struggles with and against the city of Detroit to better understand who we were and to fashion a new sense of self. We were both looking for answers, even when we didn't always know the questions. It was a heady time that often occurs in one's life, when the old scripts become played out, and new ones are required. We were fortunate to encounter Detroit in this period because the city was, despite or perhaps because of its problems, the perfect place for self-exploration. We were also fortunate to discover each other. *Kick Out the Bottom* is an experiment itself, in keeping with the sort of revelations we discovered in the city. It is a hybrid, collaborative memoir written by two people whose experiences often overlapped. While we don't always agree on the meanings we found, we are united in our appreciation of Detroit at that crucial moment in our lives.

This book is also a chronicle of our mutual friend, inspiration, and guide, Ryan. It was Ryan who gave the book its title. Riding through Detroit in his car, I was explaining my frustrations and lamenting my inability to break old patterns when he turned to me with his characteristic innocence and announced: "Instead of struggling to escape, why not kick out the bottom, and emerge through the other side?"

Ryan was a unique and exceptional individual, and the catalyst for many of the changes that we underwent while living in Detroit. While most people develop their persona in their teen years and often stick with it the rest of their lives, Ryan was constantly mutating, shifting personas to suit the particular purpose. By turns mystic, guru, scholar, punk, anarchist, shaman, magician, lover, and fool, he was always there for us, and always an inspiration. Everyone has probably encountered such a person at some point in their lives, someone whose life outside the margins of conformity and expectation invite us to reconsider our own direction through the universe. By no means perfect, he was nevertheless always sincere and earnest, and became a beacon for anyone interested in questioning their life. The answers he provoked were different for everyone, but there were common denominators that formed the core of his "teachings." While he ironically never lived in Detroit himself, he was often exploring it with us, and his ideas left an indelible mark on how we interpreted what we saw.

This book is an attempt to come to terms with both Ryan and the city of Detroit. We were lucky enough to experience both, and since then both have become our muse, friendly haunting, and perhaps even guardian angel. We knew Ryan and Detroit about as well as anybody could, and seek to resurrect them, along with our own ghostly selves, among and between the lines of these pages. We offer this modest account in the hopes of an uncanny resurrection of specters that, for both of us, are still very much part of our lives. The events of which we speak happened in a past, a past still alive but, nevertheless, still a past. This work seeks a new tense, one that looks backwards but strives to contain a lost moment's impact as it bleeds into the present tense of the telling.

Arise, spirit, arise within us, commune, and tell us the truth about what we think we know...

I

EM

My first experience of Ryan occurred in a classroom. I had just arrived in Detroit from Missouri in 1997 in order to do graduate work at Wayne State University. I had completed my master's at the University of Missouri and, despite the positive experience, I wanted to push my work further. By all accounts my new advisor, Barrett, was the mentor I was looking for, an intense individual with a comprehensive knowledge of 20th century American literature as well as a strong background in theoretical concerns. Missouri was steeped in the 19th century, a genteel department that had taught me a lot but that had started to feel a bit provincial. A new teacher in a new city, I hoped, would offer fresh perspectives, and fresh challenges.

I had only spoken with Barrett once over the phone. When I got to Detroit I immediately enrolled in his graduate theory course. I still remember the first day of class. I was nervous—I had just uprooted myself in order to come to Detroit, a city that seemed hollowed out and dysfunctional. There were no hallmarks of the "city" as I had come to know growing up in the San Francisco Bay Area: no coffeehouses, no used bookstores, no vibrant street life. I had not only uprooted myself, but my girlfriend Julie as well, who was struggling with what to do in a city neither of us had ever been to before. So when I walked into the class, I wondered what was in store for me, my relationship, and my career. I sat down and hoped it would all work out somehow.

I wasn't disappointed. The class was a breath of fresh air. The readings were stimulating, and the discussions intense. I found it a heady mix, a space where I could rethink the ideas I had absorbed, accumulated, and constructed over the course of my life. It was a crucible where the dross burned away, replaced by new possibilities of thought. But as important as that first encounter was, the memory of the course will always be connected with my memory of meeting Ryan.

My first impression of Ryan was generated by two complementary traits: his eagerness and his sincerity. You could see a hunger in his eyes, a desire to engage the world around him. As time wore on, I came to better understand the nature of this desire, but at this point the force struck me more than the quality. Ryan's inquisitiveness manifested itself in class immediately. It became instantly clear to me that I was not dealing with just another graduate student in English. The nature of his questions, and the intense feeling behind them, spoke to another type of character. Most successful graduate students realize that literary study is not just about reading books, but about mastering a way of talking about texts that enters into dialogue with those more advanced in the field. Ryan was completely oblivious to this aspect of graduate study. The texts were there as a catalyst for his own inquiries (though they were unknown to me at this time) rather than as material to be parlayed into a career.

I immediately admired him for this, since it was very close to my own feelings. As an undergraduate student at UC San Diego, I had become interested in Beat writers like Jack Kerouac and Allen Ginsberg, in part because of their connection to my hometown. But I was mainly drawn to the ways that their work chronicled experiments in living. I became fascinated by how they tried to live spontaneously in the moment, and the possibilities and problems that such immediacy created for both their lives and their writing.

My dissertation came to focus on how the Beats "captured" the moment, but I didn't want to emulate their findings—I wanted to conduct my own experiments in order to find out who I really was, and what I really believed to be true.

CK

Ryan and I met at a movie theater in the suburb of Sterling Heights, a consumerist wasteland on the outskirts of the metro area. It was more populated, even bloated, compared to what happened on the city side of 8 Mile Road.

The theater rested inside the bowels of Lakeside Mall, a white-blight monster on Hall Road, otherwise known as 20 Mile Road. The movie house was even stranger than the capitalist hell surrounding it. Because the suburbs were uneventful for teenagers, this down-and-out multiplex attracted every eccentric within twenty miles.

I had worked there six months, and it was Ryan's first day. We were both sixteen or seventeen, and Detroit natives. We exchanged glances and shook hands as the shift leader informed me that I'd be training him.

Our first task involved crossing the mall to borrow ice from another vendor because our machine broke earlier that evening—a common occurrence for the failing theater. At a Friendly's restaurant, we scooped ice for several moments in silence. Then, I looked up at him with exasperation, making sure he knew we needed to lug these heavy buckets across the mall and back to the theater. He smiled with a lopsided smirk, which charmed me but seemed unnecessary for the mundane task. Looking back, this playful grin became one of his trademarks. It conveyed a secrecy, like amusement for a joke untold.

I liked him immediately.

Even then, his aura sparkled, but maybe I didn't notice how bright it was, or maybe he hadn't developed what it would become in later days. Nevertheless, he was a curious man with bright eyes who assessed everything like a child, and as I studied him, I imagined his middle-aged self would look the same. An outsider at heart with an ageless incorruptibility, his magical nature struck me even then. Not because he was a misfit like the other employees at the theater, but because he was smart, maybe too smart for the crowd. A darkness rested in his smile, a nightfall mystery that fascinated me, and so we became fast friends.

EM

We first spoke in the hall during a break in class. The more I talked with him, the more I realized he was entirely sincere. His highly personal approach to the material could have sounded like grandstanding, a willful negation of the profession meant to elevate himself above others. But speaking with him personally, it became apparent he was playing for higher stakes. In fact, I don't think he really cared much about what the others were doing in class. Nominally, he was getting his master's degree, but he would drop out of the program a year later to pursue his own creative writing, frustrated by the limited scope academia afforded. What he was really doing was obvious—following his own mind, his own interests, and his own preoccupations.   Most of my friends at Missouri were savvy about their careers. I wasn't. First and foremost for me was the research, the writing itself. I wanted to explore the Beat writers, and the university was a means of support. Having spent several years after my undergraduate days as a writer in a Bay Area tech company, I was tired of doing what I should do. I felt compelled to do what I wanted to do. There might not be a future in it, but for the present, it was enough. Ryan understood.

This sincerity he had, this openness to others, was the main attraction that drew me to him. It didn't hurt that I found the ways he used the material from class to be intellectually stimulating. Nor that our intellectual interests often overlapped. Or even that each one of his ideas seemed to inspire several new ones in my own head. These were important facts that no doubt cemented our friendship and kept us calling each other to meet up at a coffee shop or driving around in his car to talk, talk, talk. But none of this would have been possible without his underlying attitude of sincerity, of true camaraderie and openness to any and all ideas, thoughts, feelings, and emotions that I might want to discuss. Anything was possible, and nothing off limits, no idea too bizarre, no feeling too personal or outrageous that it couldn't be discussed, weighed, analyzed. It was a chance to take the material of the university, the experiences I had acquired in life, the problems and the passions of my existence, and make something of them greater than before. It was an opening to think anew.

Our shared class ended, but our discussions went on, and a new type of education began.

CK

Over the next ten years, we continued our friendship and, like many relationships, ours had a surface level of understanding and intimacy. But then, at age 27, I tried LSD for the first time with Ryan as my guide, and I finally understood that mystery behind his enigmatic smile. Peaking on the Lysergic Acid, his camouflage dissipated, and a rawness, an almost eternal quality, overtook his features. I comprehended his entire being from this one look, and all things, every mystery kept close to his vest, became accessible. Ryan's multifaceted personality could shift, conveying different characters to different people. Individuals often perceived him based upon their own understanding of themselves and where he fit into their lives, so he became my spiritual guide. In that moment, I understood his darkness. I understood what he called magic. I understood his struggle. It became obvious why he fought against society. His outlook was mystical, but modern living didn't allow room for that crap, and contemporary people didn't make room for him. How frustrating this must have been for him, for everyone to always question his motives (myself included). Yes, I met him all over again, but this man wasn't boyish like the individual I met at the theater. This man was a wizard who concealed magic behind a level of understanding difficult for me to articulate. His smokescreen diverted the curious, and he liked it that way.

After this second introduction, our friendship changed. Before, we were comrades who shared similar interests at a superficial level. Later he became a mentor concerning mysticism. He never instructed per se. Ceremonial magic, his specialty, remained his thing, a secrecy. I had to crack that nut on my own. No, he didn't teach. He led by example. Illuminating ideas through his own actions and behavior, he showed me how to tap into the universe in a way I thought was impossible. And we did this, in a kind of love, like poets searching for transcendence.

EM

In every life there are periods when change becomes possible. For whatever reason—a breakup, a move, a chance change in the weather—something in life opens up and admits a new possibility. I encountered Ryan during one of these periods. Graduate school taught me a lot, but I still hadn't answered the larger questions. Who am I? Why am I here? Where am I headed? When I first went to college, I assumed that I would be told, and sought meaning in all of my courses. But I soon realized the university was better at posing questions and discussing possible solutions than in actually solving them. Ironically, asking about the ultimate meaning of life was seen as naive. As time passed, I read widely, pondered deeply, and filtered the world around me, hoping that there was something I had overlooked. I had always been a seeker, but by the time I reached Detroit, the search felt thwarted. The power to just leave, walk out on your identity, and start fresh. That's what he promised, and it was enticing.

EM

When I first arrived in Detroit, I didn't settle in the city immediately. Instead, Julie and I found a place in a suburb called Oak Park, just north of the city. It was the most respectable place we could find, given the money I received from my fellowship. But it was not ideal. Oak Park felt unsettled. It originally hosted a Jewish community, but as they moved west to greener pastures a Black community moved in to take their place. It was a neighborhood of strivers, of middle-class African American life climbing north out of a deteriorating city, and our brick row of town homes provided a modicum of respectability for those who could not afford a stand-alone house. We felt boxed in, surrounded by less-expensive homes we still couldn't afford on two sides, and by a struggling strip mall that miraculously failed to offer anything we wanted to buy. And our last border was 10 Mile Road, a large street fronting the highway that offered egress in only one direction: east.

A feeling of displacement permeated the complex. People weren't dissatisfied so much as unsatisfied, and restlessness prevailed. The parking lot provided a telling example. Every night would find at least one resident sitting in their car, listening to music at a high volume. I had never seen this phenomenon before and pondered why someone would leave a perfectly good home to sit in their car in a cold Michigan winter. But I soon realized that it was because there was nowhere else to go. Lacking a bar, café, or restaurant (or the funds to sit in one of them), residents found that the most convenient place to seek solace was in their vehicle, that omnipresent symbol of Detroit. Cars often became the third bedroom, that extra space lacking at home that bled out into the parking lot. Stereo systems were installed that surpassed anything indoors.

It didn't take me long to discover the probable source of these vehicular meditations. As Julie and I began to argue, I realized the value of having more space. They were the fights and squabbles of any relationship, it's true, but I began to see how my growing unease and dissatisfaction infected the relationship. The fights began over space itself; who got the little upstairs room, who was assigned to the basement, where things went. But physical space was just the pretext, the placeholder, for the real disagreement over what I saw as a need for more metaphysical space. I felt stifled, penned in, and longed for the freedom to search for something else. Independence. Or at least independence from the sort of dependence that I reflexively sought over and over and over again in relationships.

I had gotten myself into a pattern of supportive unions that were a means of not addressing my own feelings, problems, and desires. Not to say that every one of my romantic involvements were unrewarding or mired in dysfunction. I enjoyed many beautiful moments and have fond memories of each. But relationships were a crutch. By focusing on someone else, I conveniently avoided dealing with myself. My partner could be counted on to offer solace and support as I deferred issues to another day, or they could be blamed as the cause for the problems that were, in the end, rightfully mine alone.

Many of us perform a version of this play in our lives, and I am not claiming to be special or unique. But with the coming of Ryan, I began to take a closer look at the scripts I neurotically played out over and over in the course of my romantic life. The more I looked, the less I liked what I saw. Ryan always had a ready ear and knew when to listen and when to interject. There are always friends to hear you out, and most often they fall into line with your views. Ryan, however, pushed further. While he was sympathetic, he was also brutally honest. For him it was never a question of right and wrong, who was the aggressor and who the victim. He couldn't care less about assigning blame. What mattered was becoming aware of what you were doing, how you were reacting, finding out why, and most importantly, doing something about it. The solution was simple—all that was necessary was to find out what you wanted to do and do it. Who said what, who started what, who was at fault—that was all just noise. If you were honest with yourself, remained true to your own desires, and admitted those desires honestly to your partner, then everything else followed. Relationships faltered, ironically, because people did not listen to themselves enough. Of course, mutual respect and care for your partner and their thoughts was essential as well. But ultimately, everyone needed to be honest with themselves first.

But how do you do that?

Detroit came to represent that desire for a new start. I needed a transitional space, a clearing, where I could reassess both myself and my direction into the future. Ryan never suggested moving. That was not his style. How could you discover yourself if someone was constantly telling you what you should do? But I could see that Detroit would offer a chance to be alone. It offered the space I needed if I was ever going to develop an independent sense of self that would underwrite the rest of my life.

Julie understood but was understandably frustrated. Like many of the women I would come to be with, she respected Ryan's intelligence and motives, but felt that his approach was a bit too self-centered. Was it really about a search for self, or a convenient means of justifying selfish motives? We debated this often, and I could certainly see her point. Yet it was undeniable that our relationship had been struggling even before Ryan's arrival. Her inability to settle into a routine only exacerbated an already difficult situation. We split up.

So as our year lease ended, I left Julie and Oak Park, and took a cheap basement apartment in Detroit, a few blocks away from the university. And a new life began.

CK

It was an unpopular idea among whites like me to take the plunge and move into Detroit's inner circle with its crackheads, thugs, abandoned buildings, and wildlife. I welcomed its lessons because I needed to metaphorically die. I needed to enter what the theologians referred to as the "dark night of the soul." My marriage to Gayle had ended the previous year, and this crisis challenged my preconceptions about personal responsibility. Our seven-year relationship was formative, but the divorce delivered a low point. I wanted to commit suicide but didn't have the courage, so I tackled a bankruptcy both moral and financial. Detroit became perfect for this transformation because it allowed seclusion for a moment of monastic life. I needed time to reflect. Moving into the dangerous area of the Cass Corridor added an element of chaos that was needed to shake me up. Detroit became the perfect vehicle to support this awakening because we had kinship—the city and I were both down and out, in need of regeneration.

EM

Detroit was an evacuated city. People blamed the urban uprisings of 1967 when the raid on an unlicensed bar (called a "blind pig") by white cops in a Black neighborhood sparked a five-day spree that some called a "riot" and others a "rebellion," depending on the color of one's skin. But the city's racial problems were deep-seated. A 1943 riot pitted white Detroiters against Black citizens who had the "audacity" to try and move into all-white neighborhoods. White flight started soon after, with the city's white population falling

95% from 1950 to 2010. By 2000, 82% of the city was African American. The overall population began to dwindle too, from a high of almost two million in 1950 to roughly half of that in 2000. Today, that number is under 700,000.

Detroit's land area, however, has stayed the same, at 143 square miles. Unsurprisingly, this exodus left the city looking haggard. Things just weren't kept up, and the blocks that remained occupied battled against the outlying wastes where drugs, violence, burned-out homes, and a general feeling of entropy and decay crept closer every week. At least outwardly.

However, the situation also created possibilities. Not the least important was that the rents were low. There was a cost to living in Detroit. Hands were always out begging for a quarter, a dime, some change. You paid more for eggs and bread at the liquor stores that were left, and the quality was lower. Everything was inconvenient, and if anything got done, it was done in a slipshod fashion. Customer service was brusque. It was the sort of place where it took several extra steps to do anything, from registering your car to buying a broom. But the rent was cheap, and if you were willing to take the bus north to forage in a better suburban grocery store, you could survive on very little.

We were interlopers. Carpetbaggers. Whites from positions of privilege who could always leave. That dichotomy created understandable friction. As a graduate student living close to Wayne State, I had a legitimate reason for being in Detroit. But despite the generally positive acceptance I experienced from the African Americans I met, there was always a small undercurrent of suspicion. And rightly so. If I was stuck in a city with few ways out, I too would be wary of those looking for the "experience" of Detroit, regardless of how well-intentioned they might be. Walking the streets as a white man, I always felt this duality tugging at me. It produced a type of schizophrenia to always be wondering what others, the majority in this case, were thinking about you. Just like Black Detroiters must feel crossing 8 Mile into the white suburbs.

CK

Detroit attracted various people for various reasons. Artists came for the large warehouse spaces available for workspace, as did musicians for practice areas. One could rent a flat or apartment for between $300 and $500. This made Detroit a destination for artists from other more expensive cities like New York, Los Angeles, and Chicago. They also used the cheap apartments and houses near the Cass Corridor, Woodbridge, Hamtramck, Mexicantown, and Corktown. People would live four or five to a space, making the rent $100 per person.

Bohemians like writers, painters, performance artists, and musicians filled these cultural areas. This created a lively underground. Murals meant to beautify decadence sprang up around the city. Most people had a project: a band, a movement, a cause. Something was always happening: a performance, an art show, a party.

Anarchists moved in certain circles. Most worked in the kitchens of bars and restaurants around town—a network formed beneath the surface. They worked for a few months, crashed at the Trumbullplex in the Woodbridge neighborhood (an anarchist stronghold on Trumbull Avenue), and hopped a train to a new city. A few months later, they returned with a story. Exposure to this opened my eyes to the country's real underground. When I was a suburbanite, I had no connection to this way of life, but I learned much from them, and I even adopted some of their political views.

Students and professors also lived in these areas because they wanted to be near Wayne State University and the Center for Creative Studies, both located in the cultural area near the Detroit Institute of Arts. Many professors were transplants from other cities. Students came down from the suburbs and were astonished. These kids had never set foot in the city limits, so their shock was palpable.

The restaurant and bar scene had many flavors. For conversation, brunch and a Bloody Mary: the Cass Café or the Majestic Café. For an upscale dinner and cocktails: Union Street Saloon. For bowling and PBRs: the Garden Bowl. For local rock n' roll shows: the Gold Dollar, Paycheck's, Smalls, or PJ's Lager House. For late-night flirtations with oblivion: the Bronx Bar, Jumbos, or Third Street Saloon. For the last stop of goth dancing and shots: City Club. And after the club: enchiladas in Mexicantown. Most of these places were dives or had historical significance, and despite the city's abandoned appearance, it was truly alive at all hours.

Many tiers of artists and galleries existed. The people that frequented the Scarab Club were the black-tie and bleeding-heart types. They weren't the same as those who went to Detroit Contemporary Gallery with its all-night funk dance parties. The Scarab Club people were socialites who ate hors d'oeuvres and drank expensive wine. The Detroit Contemporary crowd was comprised of students and gritty artists who dealers couldn't slap in a frame and sell. Some smaller galleries tried to survive in places like the Eastern Market or Corktown. The Revolution Gallery, on the outskirts, was more for decorating upper middle-class homes.

The Russell Street Lofts held art events, but these were for the hipster crowd; a trendy DJ spun records, and you had to know somebody to get in. The abandoned Packard Plant held the progressive party/rave scene of the 90s, which led to the first Detroit Electronic Music Festival in Hart Plaza in 2000.

The isolated areas created certain scenes. The city was like a mind map, with the hub being the Wayne State Cultural Center. The other areas, like Hamtramck and Corktown, spoked out from this center. One needed a car to get to certain areas unless one wanted to ride a bike or, God forbid, walk.

Another option was the bus, but this posed its own problems. Routes went through rough neighborhoods; either the areas were dead, or they held people that didn't want you there. It became a balancing act of whether to risk taking the bus or pay for a taxi.

EM

As odd as it might sound today, Detroit has frequently been compared to Paris. Writing in 1705, Antoine Laumet de la Mothe Cadillac sung the praises of the future site of Detroit, Fort Pontchartrain, claiming that it will be the "Paris of New France" and that "all nations will come to settle there." Though French dominance would end with the French and Indian War, the reference to Paris remained. With its French architectural heritage, French street names, and Parisian-style radial avenues, Detroit would be rechristened "The Paris of the Midwest" after the British lost the city during the Revolutionary War. These allusions to the great "City of Light," though perhaps fading, can still be seen throughout Detroit, further adding to the ghost-like quality of its streets.

For those living in Detroit at the turn of our century, there was another connection to Paris. In many ways, Detroit was in its bohemian phase. Like the Left Bank in the mid-nineteenth century or Montmartre in the early twentieth, cheap rents and access to studio and recording spaces made Detroit an attractive place to be an artist. Of course, this had begun much earlier when the Cass Corridor near Wayne State University had its countercultural and artistic scenes starting in the 1960s. In some ways, that tradition remained. But with rents rising precipitously in cities like New York, San Francisco, and Chicago, suburbanites who wanted the big city experience at an affordable cost flocked to Detroit. Detroit often became a sort of bohemian way station, with artists spending a few years there developing their portfolios, then taking off to other cities to seek a wider fortune. Detroit had become "the next Brooklyn."

Detroit, however, was not Williamsburg, the Mission, or Wicker Park. Those living in the bohemian enclaves of New York, San Francisco, or Chicago could take a cheap public ride to the more established areas of the city for rest or recreation. While Detroit had venerable institutions like the Detroit Institute of Arts, the downtown was rundown and vacant, and the outlying districts inconvenient, and oftentimes downright dangerous. Like bohemians elsewhere, those in Detroit clustered in marginal neighborhoods where they were warily accepted. For Detroit, that typically meant the space around Wayne State University, where the school's amenities and police force quickly gave way to abandoned buildings, sketchy apartments, and public housing.

But like other such areas before, the benefits of affordable living and the "edge" experience outweighed the dangers of crime, blight, and inconvenience. Now that Detroit has gone through its "Revitalization," our former bohemia has become safer, hipper, and filled with the bars, clubs, and restaurants that city planners love to point to as evidence of successful renewal. Something, however, has been lost. Gone is the chance to actually engage the long-time residents of the city, as frustrating as that sometimes was. Gone is the sense that you were sacrificing the conveniences of middle-class life in order to paint, write, or study. Gone is the idea that you might actually encounter something new, different, shocking, or challenging. Gone, in sum, is bohemia.

EM

Ryan was a traveler entering the wastes of Detroit from the North, his steed a black Saturn and his cargo nothing but willingness. You could tell him instantly from the adventurers who set themselves up in the city. He stood out as "not from here," but the curious part was that he slid into the city's rhythm and vibe more readily than these pioneers did. Theirs was a grim determination, a spit-in-the-wind sort of moxie that often boiled over into an existential game of chicken. When they won, they earned bragging rights and the label "I live here." When they lost, it was not a pretty sight. The smarter ones, or at least the more careful, knew when to back off and back down. The secret to the city was invisibility and knowing when to retreat, which was often. I seldom saw him retreat though—he didn't need to, because he didn't project the image of a challenge.

Detroit intrigued Ryan, but he never let himself succumb to it. He was a suburban saint. You could not imagine him on a mountain, beard to the ground, scratching his haunches as he inspected the symmetry of a pinecone. He wasn't an urban prophet either, mumbling to himself as he walked along the street. But the suburbs? That's how he stood out so starkly. You didn't expect to find him there. Among all the debris we've come to assume as the antithesis of sainthood. Parking lots. Coney Islands. Target stores. Nobody expected to find anything there, but there he was.

The most difficult thing to reconcile with his sainthood was his car. He practically lived in his Saturn. When you climbed in you could see the evidence—coffee cups, clothes, books, CDs, and the rest of his life's paraphernalia littered the seats. How could you conceive a saint driving around the suburbs in a car? Most saints stay home, or if they do travel, it's on foot over long distances. They didn't drive while rolling a cigarette and sipping hot coffee from Tim Horton's. At least not normally.

Ryan confused everyone. He fit in everywhere, but nowhere exactly. Bred in the suburbs, he traveled through the city's wealthier outliers with a sense of familiarity. Not that he condoned what he saw. Far from it—he was fire and brimstone all the way. Ryan was like a prophet who knew that he'd find the most needful souls in precisely the worst places. That's what triggered the suspicion of his fellow suburbanites. They sensed that though he was from there and lived there, he had long ago moved away. Spiritually vacated the premises, the very place they found so comforting. But why? The question, and even more so its possible answer, disturbed them.

Eyes afire, quick with a smile, energized, never watching where he was going, Ryan moved through the world on an unplanned path, head fearlessly forward into the void.

CK

Detroit was an impractical place to live at the millennium's turn—dark and mythic with many insane challenges, a crucible of sorts. A perfect city for Ryan to troll around and find people who needed his guidance, because a clear divide existed between the suburbs and the city. This made Detroit different from other American cities: it became a duality. It was a city defined by "twos," a city with a fractured psyche and a place yearning for redemption, trying desperately to merge its disparate halves.

Ryan wasn't like the usual city people. Nor was he like the suburbanites. Both personas struggled against each other. A pull between safety and freedom. He balanced in the center fighting against both currents but at the mercy of neither—a traveler in both, like the image of The Magician in Aleister Crowley's *Book of Thoth* tarot deck, balancing on the tip of a surfboard with chaos in its wake.

He wasn't attractive in the usual sense, but he had an inquisitive manner with the magnetism of a leader. He stood tall and thin with long arms. His utilitarian fashion consisted of a plain black t-shirt, faded blue jeans, and combat boots. Mousy brown hair swept back across his forehead created a timeless style, and that lopsided Iggy Pop grin conveyed an almost reptilian-quality that pervaded his movements and facial expressions. His eyes were his most striking feature. They carried the dignity of a wild animal, an inherent wisdom. Eyes that shifted from warm and inviting, to cold and almost heartless. A friend labeled them "Jesus Eyes" because of their intensity; they misled the curious like gargoyles who scared casual visitors from the secrets of the inner temple. Looking at his aura, it seemed his soul might burst from his body. It might have been the caffeine and nicotine addiction, or his other habit—his antinomian battle with himself. Either way, health radiated from the man, but he also seemed under the thumb of something, free yet bound.

With a *Felix the Cat* tattoo on his shoulder, he often went shirtless while "in the zone." He exuded sex appeal. Men and women competed for his attention. This was obvious when he entered a party . . . his presence polarized the crowd. He drew intellectuals and seekers to him. People who feared their own power hated him. They either avoided the man altogether, or took their advantage by attacking him. He wasn't the guy who hung out in a corner. He demanded more.

Our friendship was complicated. First and foremost, Ryan will always be my brother. He exposed me to esoteric knowledge I hungered to learn more about. We became rivals in some ways, and at times, even enemies. While partaking in each other, it became difficult to retain individuality. This happens in most romantic relationships, but this became the first and only friendship where I felt it. We orbited each other. I thrived off the occult knowledge he revealed. He thrived off the energy of my mutation. We exchanged literature and ideas. Explored the mind. Shared lovers. Experimented sexually. Anything to break the barriers.

He affected outsiders profoundly, cutting through them like an ocean liner cuts through water. He was the bow, the fulcrum, the pivot point, sending a wave in either direction. Left side of the bow wave, people tumbled away unaware; those who didn't understand his teachings because they didn't have enough latitude. They saw a fool. Right side of the bow wave, people crushed under the wake; those whom the corporate propaganda-machine mesmerized. . . . His presence reminded them of their own doubt. On the middle point, balancing on oblivion's tip, stood the scarce seekers trying to break free of limitations. They became his magicians.

CK

He often came to my apartment on Prentis within the Cass Corridor, a rough place as one drifted away from the cultural area around Wayne State. My tenement sat on the zone's edge, so I rarely came into contact with the pushers, prostitutes, and whack-jobs who hung around that end of the street. But I wasn't immune to these people. A slumlord owned my building, so rent stayed cheap. Many occupants smoked crack and shot heroin. Most days in the hall, I smelled drugs cooking from a tenement room. Sometimes, I entered the building, and the sour body odor of a crack-smoke bouquet nearly made me vomit.

The building endured for so long that the wood moldings became petrified. The tannins bled to the surface, mixed with the cigarette and crack smoke, and blended with the building's age. This caused a chemical reaction, where the wood transmuted to resemble a geode's inner section—browns, yellows, reds, and greens swirled in a fossil of antiquity and process. The hallway carpet became worn into a greasy plastic smear. The trail recorded the past; a footstep culmination of 1950s autoworkers, trampled by flower children who endured the 1968 uprising, and buried by the dirty footprints of drug addicts who now claimed ownership over the building. Surrounded by the undead, I walked this path often feeling like the protagonist in Richard Matheson's *The Last Man on Earth.*

The walls had a yellowed, milky glaze. Most windows had cracks. My apartment's interior looked like the rest of the units, although mine contained modest furniture, a futon, and a bookcase. Other units were lucky if they had a ratty box-spring. My creative supplies and paintings piled up in the living room.

Cockroaches ran everywhere. I slept with the lights on, but this never helped. I often woke to a scurrying noise, or one crawling in my hair. I never used the kitchen, for fear of more infestation. I put containers of red wine in strategic places to trap the bastards, but this made little impact on their population.

My back window faced the Bronx Bar, and the sounds of reveling came through until the wee hours of the morning. . . . I remained alone. Occasionally, screaming came from upstairs. . . . Not death shrieks, but tormented wails from heroin withdrawal. Still, I remained alone. These screams and revelries just confirmed my isolation. My solitude became a prison where only I knew the boundaries, and that made me more isolated. At least the drunks had other drunks. The addicts had other addicts.

The property manager never concerned himself about when I'd pay rent, because I was the only tenant with a J-O-B. I was a loner. I never smoked crack. I never hung out on the front porch like Harvey Keitel's character in *Taxi Driver.* I never made a noise, because all my electrical equipment—my stereo, my television, my computer—shorted out in a power surge. An event Ryan called synchronicity. The universe always provided what one needed, and synchronicity connected incidents by causality and meaning—the universe's language. Ryan championed this theory. No coincidences in life. Never. No accidents. Here, the universe decided I didn't need television anymore, so I read more books.

I passed other tenants each day in the hall, and I imagined what they must have thought of me. I was the alien here. Now and then, one struck up a conversation as I exited the building. At first, I remained polite. But they soon asked for money. A game of how-to-leave-the-building-without-anyone-noticing ensued. I waited for the coast to be clear. I put my ear to the door. Sometimes, I waited for almost an hour because I didn't want to deal with these people. The longer I lived there, the more they pressed for money. I was paying rent, so they knew I had that damn J-O-B.

EM

I moved into an apartment walking distance from the university. My fellowship stipulated that if I lived in university housing the rent would be half. So, it was $182 a month, utilities included. That was the upside. The downside was that it was a basement apartment, and my windows faced the alley. I had a view of the dumpster and I could see the weeds shooting up from the pavement in the summer and the snow drifting against my window in the winter.

It was a railroad apartment that ran the length of the building. In the back there was a walk-out sunk into a stairwell. When I first arrived, I was greeted by a human turd lying ominously in the bottom landing. I stepped over it and put the key in the door.

The apartment was redeemed by a long row of windows and the fact that I could exit via the back without climbing through the basement stairs to the building's main entrance. I only used that entrance a few times, mainly when I retrieved mail once a week. There was a clawfoot tub that I would sink into in the colder months. Gazing up through a grilled bathroom window, I would watch the waning light filter through and sometimes catch the shadow of a rat scurrying along the brick siding.

It wasn't much, but it was mine and it was cheap. I set to work tidying up and making it a home in the manner of a new bachelor. I can't say it became a palace, but it was livable, and I did pass many joyful days, and even some blissful ones. Of course the darkness did seep in. To maximize light, I kept the shades open, but that meant anyone could see into the apartment. So I slept in a large windowless room. It offered a deep sleep, but my dreams were not always pleasant.

Outside was another matter. The stairwell gave out to a small backyard. There was a bit of lawn with a picnic bench. A crabapple tree grew in the corner. I was surprised how little this area was used, but I made the most of it. I would also spend time on my stairwell, a sort of reverse stoop where I would drink coffee in the morning or read in the afternoon. Because this was one of the few areas where the old brick buildings survived, the view from the stairs was actually quite nice if you liked Midwestern cityscapes— alleys behind three story tenements and wooden fire escapes climbing the walls like vines.

There weren't many of us, and not many places to go. A few bars, a few restaurants, a liquor store, and if you wanted fresh vegetables, a tolerable market within a reasonable walk. And for me there was the campus, with libraries and books and an all-night study area. But these limitations helped form a community, and I developed friends quickly.

CK

A desolate city, Detroit was perfect for Carl Jung's psychological individuation. Its mythic quality recalled stories of heroes who journeyed into dark underworlds or fierce jungles. In Ryan's words, I "entered the ruins" to take part in an archetypal voyage to attain the mythical Golden Bough, a gift to Proserpina, the queen of Pluto, king of the underworld. Like a dying god who sacrificed himself to revive a kingdom, like Bacchus with his pinecone staff, I needed death and rebirth. In our many conversations, we discussed delving into my psyche's darker regions, into the underworld. He led me deeper by allowing me to lead. A Zen chaperone who always answered a question with another question. Some said a guru, but that sold him short: too many negative connotations. Catalyst might be a more appropriate title. Psychopomp, a term used in occult texts, works better though—a mysterious figure leading the innocent to self-realization and wisdom. Hermes. Mercury. Thoth. A figure who takes risks balancing on the edges of chaos, magic, and oblivion. All in the name of mutation. Ryan presented a metaphysical mirror. Like Perseus's polished shield, he helped me to see my self's darker reflection, and I became a seeker attuned to my own power.

Near the middle of my year lease on Prentis he came down from the suburbs more. Since that LSD trip, his curiosity concerning my progress became more intense. Each night he swung by and said, "Man, I don't know how you're doing this. I gotta hand it to you. It takes major balls to live in a place like this." I shrugged it off. It was the right place to be, at least for now.

One night, the entire building almost burned down. Again, Ryan's synchronicity was at play. I sat with him drinking coffee at the Cass Café, a local hangout that drew the city's disparate factions together. One could find Wayne State professors grabbing lunch, the poets John Sinclair and Ron Allen sipping a drink, anarchists washing dishes in the kitchen, and striving garage rockers slinging cocktails. Art hung on the walls. Poetry readings brought people together. It acted as Detroit's bohemian underground, and I waited tables there.

But that night, I was off work. As we headed back to my tenement, sirens filled the night. We rounded the corner in a hurry and saw smoke. Flames consumed the third floor. Someone lit a mattress on fire and threw it down the back stairwell. The firemen took an axe to my door because nobody answered their knock. Detroit's Finest put out the fire quickly and saved the rest of the building. Perhaps they should have let it burn: one less delinquent building to worry about. Post-haste, I developed carpentry skills because a gaping, man-sized hole in my door would not go away. I screwed a plywood board over the hole. It stayed that way for months, and every night I worried that one of America's Most Wanted would rob or kill me. After a lot of pestering, the landlord finally replaced the door.

Time passed in silence and I learned more about myself meditating on my life. I sat inside my pseudo-monastery waiting for something to happen, for me to become whole again.

EM

Ryan was my spiritual guide, but he was by no means perfect. He was, for example, a man of infinite contradictions. When I first met him, he had a beat-up 1987 Ford Ranger "held together," he once said, "by a few rust patches and a Mercury Rev sticker." He traded that in for a new Saturn, telling me how impressed he was when the salesman had him jump up and down on the car's door in the showroom. Ryan was the ultimate commuter, logging hundreds of miles around the city, even though he usually drove without a destination in mind. Given that his mind, body, and soul were constantly in motion, the car seemed merely a necessary dermis that enveloped him during his daily and nightly wanderings. Yet the paradoxes this vehicle involved him in were endless. The gas it required, the insurance he had to pay, its exhaust, and the weight of its responsibility seemed the farthest thing from his world. Nevertheless, it was always there, implicating him. But these contradictions also served a pedagogical function. They taught you how to question the unstated assumptions that governed your entire life.

When we first started hanging out, I was surprised to find that he wanted to meet in a chain coffee shop. How could such a man, a man with such talent, frequent an insipid, boring, commercialized establishment with tacky wall ornaments and institutional floor tiling? How could he be served from the standard round glass coffee pot with a black plastic rim? Shouldn't he be at an upscale café among a bohemian set in the city's hipper suburbs? But there he was, never eating, getting his coffee refilled as he pored over another volume of philosophy, ready at a moment's notice to jump into his Saturn when he felt stasis, blockage, or just an urge to move.

CK

Because of my renunciations, I shirked a phone. When I needed one, I used the rickety payphone at the end of the street in front of the liquor store. I tried to make my call before the inevitable homeless man asked for money. I was using a pay phone; I had change. Whatever business I attempted became more complicated when waving away someone calling me an "a-hole" for not giving them money. Frequently, I was on an important call with a supervisor or a government clerk while I was telling someone to get lost as they were saying, "Go fuck yourself, honky."

I hoped and prayed that talk remained talk, and did not turn into something sinister. Whatever way one lived in the city, the constant threat of petty crime influenced decisions, and I can only imagine what it was like for a woman. Questions like these came to mind in a city like Detroit. If I carry a large TV box into the apartment, will I come home to find my new TV stolen? If I stay out too late at a friend's house, should I crash there instead of walking home? Should I keep my wallet in my left pocket and stuff decoy money in my right pocket, so if robbery ensues I can drop the decoy and sprint?

Ryan had the luxury—as did many other friends—to come down and visit without experiencing many of Detroit's frustrations. It wasn't like they were immune. People asked them for money too, but it was different. When you lived there, immersed in the chaos, no escape presented itself. On more than one occasion, I saw Ryan pull a Jedi Mind Trick on someone trying to mess with him—a cunning misdirection by answering a question with another question. If a homeless man asked for money, Ryan might answer with "What happened to your family?" or "How did you get here?" By the time the homeless man finished answering, they had forgotten the initial question concerning money. I learned a lot from these moments. Distraction was better than frustration.

EM

If there was one word that guided Ryan, it was "Will." He often quoted Aleister Crowley's dictum, "Do what thou wilt shall be the whole of the law." The word is so slippery, and I often found myself struggling to grasp its meaning. "Will" here, as he often reminded us, was not simply desire, though it was embedded in a larger interpretation of the concept. Crowley was not advising, "do (whatever) you want," or at least not solely advising that. They both argued, instead, for an expanded notion of "Will." Not simply desire, or compulsion, but a sort of informed intention. One born of necessity? Yes, necessity, but not necessity as constraint; more of an expression of innermost soul, essence, "Will" in an earlier, Enlightenment sense. Nietzschean, but not exclusively, since, to my mind at least, Nietzsche was actually not subtle enough here. And not Schopenhauerian either, with his pessimism. "Will" as forceful action, but emanating from a calm, still personal core that guaranteed (without need for conscious thought) the resulting event would be conducted in accordance with an established confluence of being. A marriage of being and becoming. Action as the manifestation and guarantee of being in such a manner that it appeared natural, evident, necessary, and dare I say it, "right."

It would be easy to point to the litany of philosophy, theology, and myth that says much the same thing. He was versed in that too, and had all of these texts—and many, very many more we'd never heard of—at hand. But he was the first person I'd ever met that truly embodied them. And not as some walking compendium, or self-conscious demonstration. He had truly folded these texts, their words and their ideas, into himself. At his most self-conscious moments they would erupt and become discernible—a Nietzschean decision, a Bhagavad Gita-en renunciation, and so forth, but most often they would blend seamlessly with the self that came to the foreground. Not an avatar, not an example, but a man who truly knew how to turn philosophy into practice—and without the false dichotomy that this all-too typical separation implies.

During one of Barrett's classes we were reading about Niklas Luhmann's idea of systems theory. Ryan picked up on the idea of each system having a blind spot, and from there began talking about how if each system could be made to cover another system's blind spot, you could per-haps develop a better, or even a "final" system. I mentioned Michael McClure's idea of a "systemless system" that I read about in *Scratching the Beat Surface*, and Ryan began playing around with this idea. Could you design a system that wasn't bound by the limitations of traditional structures? A "system" in name only, that mutated as needed to perform a set of changing functions? Most of the students seemed puzzled by Ryan's ideas, but I recall our professor being intrigued.

His will was his guide, and it allowed him to sift through the world's offerings, taking what was useful and abandon-ing what was not. Ryan took much from philosophy, but his omissions were telling. Take, for instance, Hans-Georg Gadamer's concept of the "Horizon," defined as the range of vision from a particular vantage point. Some students were interested in the idea as a means of thinking through possibilities and how they could be formulated, but Ryan never bothered with the concept. He heard it enough in our class, but never picked it up. Why would a horizon mean nothing to him? Because it represented a limit, and Ryan was always trying to move beyond? I was fixated on the future, on trying to make what I wanted to happen happen. But Ryan was more concerned with perpetual possibility. The present was sufficient. "You're a star," he would say, pointing at my chest. He collapsed the horizon to a point.

He bristled whenever our discussions threatened to fall into dichotomies. The world was energy, attention, will, and not a grid that would suffer linear plottings and diametric solutions. Undifferentiation was his rule and ruler. He hated dialectics, dualisms, binary decision-making. The either-or. Small wonder he was reticent about the computer, though he pragmatically embraced it as a tool. He was the great transcender.

CK

He read and experienced everything he could. This put him in a space where other people seldom ventured—an outlander. He knew secret connections between things. For him, reading an engaging novel became a connecting of the dots, with every other writer leaving clues toward the grand puzzle. Experiences, experiments, information, and magic become a limitless interconnected tapestry. He gleaned knowledge from everywhere: high and low literature and art, the media, secret societies, his friends and enemies. Threads came from everywhere. Literature lessons bled into magical secrets, and vice versa. The discovery of global domination by occultists complemented his interest in Outsider Art. Yoga harmonized with his attraction to philosophy. By listening to the universe, by hearing its voice, he understood the transcendental aspects that many artists and magicians tried to relate. It's as if the various forms of knowledge elevated him higher as he made correlations between subjects as advanced as ancient Egyptian magic, and something as mundane as a certain brand of beer. To him, the symbols became the same. Companies used sigils (magical symbols imbued with power) to sell products. These acted in the same way as the hieroglyphs Egyptian priests used to frenzy believers. He'd say, "The lie of our time is that we've accepted modernity, as if we're superior to our ancestors." He saw modernity as a prison meant to enslave us by using our pagan roots against us. He told me many times about our governmental masters who used ancient magic to influence day-to-day lives. They manipulated people through symbolism. While driving past a billboard advertising the newly built Greektown Casino, he'd say, "The enslavement depends on consumption, which depends on the consumers' ability to not believe they're being manipulated." Instead of watching the road, he told me that their slogans conveyed happiness, a feeling of well-being if we consumed products. Their logos acted as psychic buttons that hit certain parts of our brains, making us recall innate desires from early in human development. I pondered his ideas, but this led me nowhere. He concluded his thought with, "Their goal—to sell things, to damage our physical and mental processes so they can control us by making cures for diseases created from their products. It's a vicious circle where they're killing us to make room for more consumers, all the while these occultists become wealthy at the expense of the manipulated cattle they've corralled into their doom farm."

EM

Ryan's thinking also had its practical side. In addition to more spiritual matters, he was also keenly interested in the gross injustices of capitalism. It was the late-1990s, and people were beginning to understand the potential drawbacks to the emerging neoliberal order. In a globalized world where corporations made inroads into areas that were previously the domain of states and governments, the individual began to feel more and more constrained—at best an afterthought, at worst a pawn or "mark" ripe for manipulation. Ryan railed against this attack on individual thought, feeling, and expression, and one of the reasons he loved Detroit was that the corporate world had been slow to colonize it. Mom-and-pop stores like Miley and Miley Shrimp Shack, with its hand-painted sign of a smiling crustacean donning a captain's hat, were still the rule rather than the exception. He was savvy enough to see the connection between the rise of corporate influence into every aspect of daily existence, and the reliance on images that allowed this infiltration to occur. Media images drove a wedge between people and the world, leading to an ever-increasing divide between the true reality he was seeking, and a virtual realm where desires and fears were manipulated for someone else's gain. I still have a piece of writing he was working on for class that he gave to me. In it, he castigated our increasing distance from the lived world which should form the foundation for our lived lives:

If money is an abstraction of human activity—the production and consumption of goods—then credit is an abstraction of an abstraction. It is pure representation. The global information system which allows this finance capital to flow back and forth across the planet is a dead abstraction of the actual living planet. Finance capital is money which is free floating and totally autonomous like the media images that swamp us. Images without content communicating an aesthetic intensity to be uncritically consumed. We too have become objects. We create our subjectivity out of manufactured objective phenomena of the market.

A day seldom went by without confirmation of Ryan's ideas. Corporate consolidation, media proliferation, the slow reach of U.S. capitalism into every corner of the globe— Ryan's ire rose at every new bit of support for his theories. As he was often fond of saying, "Capitalism demands unlimited growth. Unlimited growth only occurs in nature as cancer."

Ryan used his understanding of magic to counter the false myths offered by an all-pervasive media culture. It was a time of "culture jamming," of Adbusters, of trying to undermine corporate culture from within. Detroit was actually ahead of the curve by being so far behind it. The city we found ourselves in felt curiously anti-capitalist. Chain stores never ventured below 8 Mile, and small shops, many with hand-painted, do-it-yourself signs were common. Ryan picked up on this. If America was awash in images meant to distract and tantalize, then why not fight image with image? Magic, with its techniques of refocusing attention through appeals to an occult world hidden behind our own, offered a means of fighting back. Ryan experimented with new myths to replace the old. In one story he gave me, the narrator imagines himself as the ghost of an Indian princess living in some far-off Latin American country. Roaming a "feverish proliferation of jungle paths," this ghost searches for the mythic creations of earlier civilizations as a means to avoid this all-consuming world of consumption. This search is fraught with peril, and its outcome uncertain. Temptation is everywhere: "There are many people I could now become. There are cultures and a billion bewildering subcultures to choose from. My head is full of the radio and the TV, magazines and movie quotations, soundbites and scraps of news, infinite descriptions, infinite explanations, infinite forms of distraction. I can cut my hair like that actress (you know the one on that sitcom) and find a billion stores to buy my lifestyle from." The bewildering array of consumer choices continually calls her away from the true world she is struggling to reclaim. In the end, Ryan is anything but upbeat, and the story concludes with the priestess's ghost beginning to doubt the quest: "There are worlds in my head, but my heart is a dark secret, and I begin to think after a while that I've never been an Indian priestess. I've always been this person I shopped for." False images have the power to trump the redemptive power of myth.

CK

Ryan's fascination with television news was one of his most consuming obsessions. Overall, I ignored the televised circus. Ryan watched it like a sociologist. He got so involved, so deep inside, that he fell into despair over his idea that "dark magicians" (his words) controlled the media. In some ways, he was right, but he had a problem separating himself from this takeover by occult means.

Despite his high intelligence, Ryan became interested in esoteric conspiracies. On one hand, being informed is necessary to living an educated life. But where does one draw the line between being informed and being manipulated? Ryan spent so much energy trying to help people see the conspiracies, that he lost much of his own objectivity. And by the ping-pong nature of his moods, one could see how deeply the media manipulated him.

Two kinds of people watch the news: those who believe in the enchantment and can't break free of it, and those who see the government manipulation in utter disbelief that this is happening repeatedly without protest. Even if one knows one is being manipulated, there's still a chance that a deeper manipulation lies below in the form of subliminal messages or magical symbols.

Therefore, the best action might be to leave the spectacle alone. I don't find myself any less informed by not watching corporate news. People talk so much about current events. I understand more by listening to them paraphrase and researching myself than by listening to some newscaster trying to convince me that Arabs are evil. In between commercials for laundry soap and hamburgers, they meddle with our emotional equilibrium. Ryan and I came to odds on this notion. He wondered how I could understand without being wired into the media. But how could he transcend the media's indoctrination? Because for me it was difficult to detach my emotions from the carnage. I couldn't observe it detached, but perhaps he could.

Countless times I met Ryan after one of his news binges drained him completely. His emotional stability plunged to a low point. He spoke absentmindedly about crooked politicians, swindles, drones, hexes, terrorist bombings, consumer manipulations, diseases, religious fanatics, plastic surgery mishaps, mass murders, and missing children. In those moments, his eyes conveyed a frustration so intense, it seemed like it might destroy him. I saw the system win by robbing his joy. This made me depressed because if the system beats a man as strong as him, what hope do we all have?

EM

Ryan could attach at will; it was the detaching that was a struggle for him. Giving so much of himself to every encounter, it was hard for him not to leave something behind. Part of his attraction to us was that we reciprocated. We formed a circuit, and fed his energy back to him. He became recharged in the process. But others less kind, or perhaps less able, or maybe just more damaged and in need of repair, saw in him a source of energy vaster and deeper than they had ever before encountered, and drank deep at his well. He was always searching for the best in someone, for that gem buried deep down that he could raise to the surface. But when it was just a chimera and he finally realized it, it was already too late.

Ryan was one of the strongest people I had ever met, but certain topics caused him no end of consternation. Politics was one example. Politics—that topic that was so passé, so uninspiring, in our bohemian circle. The topic nobody wanted to think about, much less raise in conversation. How many times would he rant, how many hours expostulate, with cigarette and coffee and one hand on the wheel? He literally could not believe what was taking place, that it was allowed to happen, that there was even debate about it. Watching him reconcile a conflict in the Middle East with the state of his soul troubled me. Not just for his sake, but for mine as well. How could he be laid so low by the daily paper, or by a drone strike so far away? Not that these events weren't troubling, but the problems they invoked for Ryan seemed to call his method itself into question. Once, as I entered his car, he asked me, "Have you heard?" I had no idea what he was talking about, and responded, "Heard what?"

He was amazed at how I could have avoided knowledge of some recent turmoil. He then calmed, turned to me, and said, "That's why you're sane."

EM

Ryan's interest in combating the power of the hostile take-over by capitalist myth would rouse him to action. This was a time when young people were challenging the new global order in direct ways. We had just witnessed a major uprising in Seattle where, in 1999, a large group of about 40,000 protestors demonstrated against the World Trade Organization meetings taking place in the city. This U.S.-led organization had routinely engaged in predatory lending practices that left many Central and South American countries slaves to America's economic policy. While protestors blocked intersections and held teach-ins, members of the "Black Bloc" smashed store windows in a defiant act against corporate culture.

Inspired by this demonstration, Ryan and I decided to head to Washington, D.C. to participate in the rallies against the World Trade Organization. During our twelve-hour drive, we talked endlessly about the Seattle riots, consumer culture, and the possible future of American capitalism. We also wondered what was going to happen in D.C., discussing the violence that occurred in Seattle and debating whether it was a useful technique in the struggle against globalization.

We arrived in a capitol that was both excited and on edge. Nobody knew what was going to happen, or what they would do when it did. We attended planning meetings, met fellow protestors, and got a firsthand look at people putting the sort of ideas we had been discussing into practice. It was an intense time filled with the inspirational and the absurd. One speaker would stir our indignation with new facts, and another would inspire our incredulity by asking whether he would be served vegan meals if he ended up in jail. In the end, we spent our time peacefully. The police had learned their lesson from Seattle, and protests were mainly subdued. Ryan and I walked the streets around the White House, meeting a wide variety of people, recording their divergent opinions on my hand-held recorder, and debriefing each other on all the ideas, feelings, and personalities that were floating through D.C. that weekend.

EM

If Ryan had an enemy, it was Fear. He struggled to banish that emotion from his existence. Virtually any other feeling was acceptable, so long as it was acknowledged and understood. Jealousy, that ugly condition, could be used to uncover latent feelings of inferiority or a desire for control. Envy could be folded back into an appreciation of covetousness and its causes. Even Anger had a place in the pantheon of human emotions, a necessary exhaust valve for venting frustration. But Fear was unproductive. It impeded without revealing. Perhaps this was because it most often came from outside, most typically a result of social programming meant to keep one on the "right" path. As someone who resisted the idea of "right" to begin with, Ryan believed in taking directions only from the self. Fear stifled exploration, and thus needed to be exiled so the search could be conducted without constraint. Once that was done, anything became possible.

CK

Ryan's magic—referred to as ceremonial magic, ritual magic, or high magic—focused on tantric exercises and working with chaos. Most people confused these arts with wizards, illusionists, and oracles. For the initiated, magic isn't the bombast of Harry Potter's Wizarding World. Or is it? Modern mythologies borrow the terminology, but their powers remain fantastical, while occultism is very real. It's not stage illusionists or Houdini either. Or is it? Illusionists draw upon occult practices to perform magic tricks. It's not fortune tellers or oracles, but occultists who summon forth the future by riding the universe's flow.

Ryan might describe it with three words: perception, presence, and ritual. The magician is a ritualist. Not just rigid Golden Dawn rigmarole, but in everyday practice. The chaos magicians of the 1980s, people like Peter J. Carroll and Grant Morrison, made every act a ritual. They performed experiments to facilitate changes in perception. Eating is a ritual. Sex is a ritual. Even breathing is a ritual. Use perception to invest each ritualized action with meaning and intention.

When Ryan told people he performed magic, they looked at him like he was insane. I was skeptical too, at first, but then I experienced it firsthand. Once, I was about to leave for a camping trip to take LSD with a few people in the forest. He didn't know about the trip, but he showed up at my house a few minutes before I left. He somehow knew. He gave me a smirk like he divined it. Did he know? How could he?

Perhaps his word choice was a semantic problem. Something like "altered consciousness" or "attuned to the moment" instead of "magic" might have created less incredulity. After knowing him, I've made sigils that influenced reality by causing events to happen. I've used techniques like fasting and sensory deprivation to alter my consciousness. Mind-altering drugs expanded my awareness. I've gained communication with my higher self, a higher part of me where I commune outside temporality through meditation and trance. All these changes in perception I owe to his influence.

Ceremonial magic is everywhere. It has many names and faces. Practitioners of every spiritual belief use these techniques to heighten their spiritual experience, and to also control others. Adepts use these same techniques to get closer to whatever god they worship. They design architecture and plan cities using occult geometry. The Statue of Liberty is Isis. Isis is Ishtar. The images and symbols go back into antiquity. Most of the great artists, mathematicians, and creators of governments use the occult symbolism. The dollar bill design drew on magical symbolism from ancient Egypt and Freemasonry, just as Hitler stole the swastika from Hinduism, Buddhism, and Jainism. All in the name of influencing consciousness. Ryan used the techniques to invest each action with meaning and intention.

EM

Few people truly know you. Sure, there are people who were there from the start: parents, siblings, relatives. They've seen you grow up and know all the stories. But their perceptions are always clouded by their own hopes, desires, and fears. Then there are the friends one accumulates along the way, and the colleagues from work. And acquaintances. But these rarely have the chance to see more than a few sides of you, and those sides are typically the ones you want to show them. Sometimes someone catches a glimpse of something deeper. But my relationship with Ryan was different. We were friends, but more than that, we shared a vision of the world that brought us together.

What Chris took from magic, I got from yoga. Ryan of course was the man who introduced me to the practice. Growing up in California, I was aware of yoga. My mother had gone a few times with her friends when I was young. But at the time I was not spiritually developed enough to understand its possibilities. Like many, I had seen it as some New Age trend, or more positively as a new type of exercise. It took Ryan to show me the significance of something that I had been aware of for years.

Ryan had only gone once or twice before. Today you can find a yoga studio in almost every part of the city, but back then the Detroit yoga scene was just getting underway. We went to a makeshift studio above a coffee shop in the hip suburb of Royal Oak. Johnny was our yogi, and I could feel when I walked in that this was a different sort of class, a different sort of space, and a different sort of teacher. Johnny exuded what I can only describe as a "strong calm." The focus was on spreading the word about yoga, and money was more of an afterthought—the class was based on donations. After briefly speaking with our yogi, we grabbed a mat and lay on the floor, ready to begin.

The class was unlike anything I had expected. As we worked through the various poses, I immediately saw what had attracted Ryan to this practice. Yoga sought to "yoke" the mind with the body through the breath. While this might have sounded overly spiritual, the results were physically perceptible. Ryan always talked about the hijacking of the word "science" by the professionals. The word now connoted a single method employed by scientists to discover rational "truth." But for Ryan, spirituality was a "science" as well, and he was indignant when people dismissed it as undisciplined. Moving through the various *asanas*, holding them, breathing, focusing on our bodies, I realized what he meant by running "experiments" on the self whose conclusions were just as important as any lab work. As he was fond of pointing out, yoga produced measurable results, even if you couldn't attach a number to them.

Looking back, I now realize Ryan was running experiments on us as well. Did he know that I would take more to yoga, and Chris more to magic? He knew I loved sports, so maybe he saw how mindfulness and getting back to the moment through an attention to the body would be the best path for me. Or perhaps he didn't know until we left Johnny's class and discussed our experience over falafel and hummus across the street. He could see what would end up being a continuing interest in yoga, and maybe even took joy in being the one who introduced me to the practice. In any case, he went on to train as a yogi, spending months poring over the sacred texts and practicing daily to prepare himself. And I think of him every time I roll out my mat and begin to move, stretch, and breathe. That shared moment of our first class stretches from that afternoon in a Detroit suburb to wherever I am at the "present" time.

CK

Knowing the universe exists as an ordered place with certain rules allowed Ryan to use these rules to gain a stronger awareness, to become more potent within sacred reality.

Writing can be magic. Letters have magical significance, as do images. Sigils work because they affect chaos. Magicians thrive there. Inside chaos, changes occur because order constrains change. Chaos allowed us to become more potent, to know ourselves more powerfully, so we could follow our True Will.

Magic becomes a contradiction difficult to describe, and convincing someone of magical reality also poses a challenge. One can't hurl fireballs on command, but then again, maybe the fire is metaphorical. One can't transform into a bat, but then again, maybe the animal is totemistic. I know that I know. I know that I don't know. I know that I know magic becomes allegory. It's all these things and none. Maybe magicians have difficulty selling the art for these reasons. We're taught as children that everything has a logical explanation, but magic isn't logical, therefore, it must not be real. But can you prove that it's not?

Ryan and I talked for hours. He tried to sell it. Time passed. He got frustrated. Was it just his inability to describe it or did I miss something? The conversation ended. Several days, or months, or even years, passed and then what he said days, months, years earlier suddenly made sense. My perception had evolved to where my mind could wrap itself around the illogical nature of the ideas. Magic is a conundrum, an enigma, a chimera. Unless one knows it, one doesn't. Unless it breathes inside one's mind, one can't understand it. And that's its mystery, and that's why it continues to thrive despite the corporate power system's attempts at containing it. It's slippery. It's a phantom. It's passed from student to teacher orally, but more precisely, it's passed by presence. Maybe this is where Ryan failed. His words didn't convince, but his presence did. Then again, maybe that was his plan all along. Maybe he knew that words were subterfuge.

EM

Ryan and I continued to explore yoga together, attending classes and discussing at length the insights we gleaned from the practice. But Ryan delved deeper. He saw in yoga a possible solution to the difficulties that were plaguing him. Yoga offered a potential to bridge the gap between mind and body, between the rational and the irrational, and between eastern and western modes of thinking that he had been struggling to reconcile for years. There was a studio in Detroit that began offering training courses for yoga instructors, and Ryan leaped at the opportunity. Convincing the studio to allow him to take the expensive six-month course at a reduced rate (and borrowing the rest of the money from his parents), Ryan began an intense course of study. Nominally, the program was designed to produce yogis who would go on to teach courses throughout Detroit and beyond, but Ryan was most immediately concerned with absorbing all he could for his own research. It was a heady mix. He would practice daily in a number of yogic traditions, then go on to study and discuss a range of classic yoga texts like *The Yoga-Sutra of Patañjali*, *The Vedas*, and *The Upanishads*. The course also included dense readings of anatomy books. I followed the course myself at a remove, reading Ryan's materials and listening to him elaborate on his findings. His excitement, and his thirst for knowledge, were contagious.

As the course drew to a close, Ryan began to attract followers. Even in the very accepting world of Detroit yoga, Ryan was an anomaly. He was respected for his intelligence and perseverance, but his intensity was not always understood. Ryan was not content to let questions go unanswered or positions unchallenged. If the teacher discussed the idea of "energy," he wanted to know exactly what they meant by the term and how they derived their understanding of it. For many in the program, the goal was to simply help others enjoy the benefits of yoga they themselves experienced. For Ryan, both the practice and the texts were a means to reach enlightenment. While this distanced him from some of his teachers and many of his fellow students, it also attracted like-minded seekers eager to study yoga through both the body and the mind.

Yoga also gave Ryan added insight into sexuality. Given his good looks and personal magnetism, he had always caught the eye of women, and quite a few men. Though he enjoyed sex and would often "hook up" with someone for the pure pleasure of the experience, sex, like everything else in his life, was really about pushing oneself to grow and mutate. Ryan's study of yoga gave his long-time interest in the flow of energies and the reconciling of opposites added impetus as he devoured sacred Tantric texts and sought others with whom he could practice implementing what he had learned.

This intense focus led Ryan to begin holding his own classes with a small group of students. The goal was to integrate the spiritual texts with the physical practice. When he described exactly what he was doing, I immediately saw the difficulty of it. Ryan gave himself—body, mind, and soul—to his pursuits, and demanded the same of his students. Not too long after his classes began, Ryan became frustrated with the lack of intensity in his charges, complaining that they were not sufficiently dedicated to the pursuit. As a teacher myself, I could see his frustration, but also the fault in his pedagogy. It is the instructor's job to slowly build enthusiasm in students by demonstrating why the material is worthy of study. Only then can the teacher slowly begin to lead the students to understanding. Ryan did not want students; he wanted fellow travelers. Going back to the beginning to explain the fundamentals frustrated him. He felt it much better to have relationships that were mutually stimulating. Teaching, however, is not simply about forging ahead. It is about slowing down to encourage someone onto the path of learning.

CK

Ryan's favorite spiritual system was Aleister Crowley's religion of Thelema (Biblical Greek for "will"). The Thelemic slogan, "Do what thou wilt shall be the whole of the Law;" to which the typical response is, "Love is the law, love under will," encapsulates the religion's basic tenets. Do what you want. Indulge in bliss. A Nietzschean or Schopenhauerian goal of doing what you desire and overcoming resistance. A universal law. Follow desire until it reveals True Will.

Ryan identified the True Will as the Holy Guardian Angel, an Oversoul unique to each individual. The main goal of the religion is to engage with this Holy Guardian Angel or Augoeides, also referred to as the radiant body. Disputes exist about what this is, but many groups including the Catholic Church, the Theosophists, the Freemasons, and the Hermetic Order of the Golden Dawn (of which Crowley was a member) searched for connection with this spiritual ideal. It goes back to Zoroastrianism and equates with the Ancient Greek idea of the "genius" or "daemon," the luminous body that breathes inspirational light into the seeker.

Thelema's goal was to conduct The Great Work, a spiritual quest to discover your True Will, your life's work, and to accomplish it. When he mentioned The Work he referred to alchemy: refining lead into gold. Similarities between alchemy and The Work become metaphorical. Those who tried to make gold from lead missed magic's point.

Ryan thought it was a break from polarities. A balance in the middle, in the moment. Yoga becomes important here. It's also very Taoist. In Crowley's book *Magick Without Tears* he writes: "The Great Work is the uniting of opposites. It may mean the uniting of the soul with God, of the microcosm with the macrocosm, of the female with the male, of the ego with the non-ego."

Ryan's interest in yoga and Eastern wisdom versus the desire-driven Thelema became a contradiction I never quite understood. In my estimation, Thelema is about ego. Many Thelemites I've met were egotists. Eastern thought abolishes ego and becomes one with the moment, one with nature. Both seem at odds, but they made Ryan who he was. A true anomaly. Someone unable to fit into either system, but striving to gain the benefits of both.

To understand Thelema one has to know about its founder. Aleister Crowley was a controversial figure sometimes known as "The Wickedest Man Alive." He developed his religion in the early 1900s after his Holy Guardian Angel, named Aiwass, contacted him and dictated *The Book of the Law* (*Liber AL vel Legis*). Crowley proclaimed himself a prophet of the new age, the Aeon of Horus. By incorporating occult ideas from the Qabalah, Rosicrucianism, yoga, and Eastern and Western mysticism, he started a new religion.

Many accounts of Crowley's life portray him as an egotist. Personally, I'm not so sure. I've done my share of reading about him, and I would say people misunderstood him. Maybe Ryan gravitated to his philosophy because they each shared an unknown quality that inspired awe in those who understood, and revulsion to those who couldn't grasp it.

Was Ryan getting his ideas from Thelema? Probably most of them, but we didn't know that at the time. In hindsight, he got his ideas everywhere. No culture or tradition or technique was off limits. However, Ryan didn't buy into these philosophies completely. With Thelema, he went to the ceremonies, and he had many Thelemite friends, but he seemed resistant to sign on completely. Ryan wasn't one of those types of Thelemites with flamboyant presentation. No frilly shirts or black bell-bottoms. No eye makeup or leather trench coat. Perhaps Ryan got through to the other side, passed that ego trap.

Ryan would never be content with any system, never content to sit on his laurels. Even if Crowley made a great deal of sense, Ryan still questioned him, looking for cracks in the philosophy. Despite being an adept and adhering to their tenets, I think deep in his heart he knew the true magician rejects dogma because it constrains consciousness. Ryan was too reflective, always critiquing the philosophy, self-critiquing, and tinkering with the system. Perhaps that's why he wanted a "systemless system." To be part of all systems but unbeholden to any of them.

Did he deviate from Crowley's ideas and was that deviation important? Yes, I think so. Crowley lived in a different time. The man was a showy individual. Ryan wasn't like that. Ryan wanted to conceal himself, to blend into different situations. His philosophy wasn't performance. Most Thelemites came across as theatrical because they use their ostentation as a weapon of influence, like Count Dracula using his powers to seduce. But that wasn't Ryan. Yes, he influenced people, but he wasn't setting out to manipulate. Sometimes, it was beyond his control. He didn't direct people toward his goals. He was fine with people doing whatever they wanted.

Did Ryan use his influence with women he wanted to bed? Who knows? Even then, Ryan wasn't about trickery, or convincing them. He was often straightforward with women. He'd say, "Hey, do you want to sleep with me?" Blunt honesty. He never maneuvered women into a room to seduce. He was a good-looking guy, so he didn't need it. If they were thirsty, they'd drink.

EM

Ryan's appearance was serendipitous. He always used to say, "The teacher appears when the student is ready." The importance of Ryan's teaching, and the reason for its influence on my life, was directly attributable to his method. The reason he never wanted the mantle of "guru" was because his teaching really didn't have a particular content. You were supposed to provide the answer; he provided guidance and support. His gift was his ability to provide a sympathetic ear that, and this was perhaps his greatest strength, was at the same time entirely honest. He inspired, advised, reflected, and refracted—he never taught.

This was a revelation. Being shy, I've never been one to have many friends, which makes the ones I have all that more special to me. Quality over quantity is my motto. In all my friendships, the ability to share heartfelt and meaningful conversation is of the utmost importance. Ryan presented an extreme example of this principle. Most friends lend a sympathetic ear, and even better ones will have the strength to tell you when you are misguided. Ryan pushed even further, providing sympathy but at the same time a completely honest assessment of your thoughts, feelings, and deeds. Even more, he pushed you to discover the underlying reasons for your choices, and to reflect on whether their results were actually what you wanted. At times this could be hard to take, but it was necessary if a true self-understanding was ever going to be achieved. And only a true sense of oneself would provide the basis for clarity and the change that can come with it.

CK

Fear. He loved using that word. He'd use it every chance he got. Fear. Fear. Fear. People fear change because it means a million possible outcomes from a comfortable position. Fear leads to metaphysical death. When you overcome fear something in you dies. Innocence. Cultural brainwashing. Ideologies. Then you're free, but freedom can be terrifying. He would say, "You can BE anything! You can DO anything!" Our society teaches us to adopt a personality, a political stance, and a profession. We need these things to feed our ego, to create an identity, and the rulers know this. That's why the magician becomes a threat. He or she shows us infinite possibilities. We have to destroy our previous self to find the truth. We have to conquer fear. Fearlessness leads to a singularity. One equals infinity. Truth equals another contradiction. Hassan-i Sabbah, founder of the Ismaili military group the Order of Assassins, said it best, "Nothing is true, everything is permitted."

EM

It was really about discovering a centered state of mind. Discovering what balance felt like, how to achieve it, and later, how to reclaim it as everything outside that stillness slowly gnawed it away, until you were back into distraction again, controlled instead of in control. Though in control was not accurate, really, since the point wasn't so much to lead oneself down a certain path through gross determination and striving, but rather, to blend with the circumstances of the world; a meshing that allowed one to exist as part of the larger flow of the universe while still maintaining a sense of self. Pure abandonment is too easy, fighting the world too difficult. A state of being perfectly in tune with the tune of the moment.

He used to speak of an incident that occurred in Northern Michigan while in college. In my mind this episode is connected with a Native American sweat lodge ceremony he participated in that summer. A tobacco ritual.

He described a man he had met in Northern Michigan who put a pistol to his head and asked, "Are you ready to die?"

Rather than put us through this trial, he instead used it to craft his own mantra, "Die Before You Die."

This phrase functioned as both admonition and *koan*, and I often thought about the price he must have paid to acquire it. And what it meant.

What did it mean? Something different for every supplicant. But to hazard an interpretation, to me it meant that one had to give up everything, all the straining and fretting and desiring, before one could truly live before the fact of death came to take it all away, anyway.

CK

Late one night, Ryan and I discussed death at The Clock Restaurant, an eatery in Hamtramck. He told me about the

Olmec game of death. The Olmec bet gold and slaves during these matches. Gambling was an integral part of the contest. Even the gambler's freedom could be collateral. Sometimes they wagered their children. He compared living in Detroit with the game. All the dangers. The chaos of the broken city. One big gamble after another. The city demanded a physical or mental death, a sacrifice.

His arms gestured wildly as he described the barbarity of the Olmec game. It was like basketball; the aim was to put the tiny ball through a stone hoop. Debates continue about what happened upon the game's completion. Some historians say the losing team sacrificed themselves because the gods didn't favor them. Therefore, they lost. Others say the winners sacrificed themselves. Victory was a quick entry into the afterlife.

He said, "Either way you cut it, the Olmec understood 'die before you die.'"

I wasn't sure what he meant, but he explained. He told me primitive man knew how to be warriors. "This world, our world, has forgotten," he whispered to himself. He took another sip of coffee, took a scan about the room, and then explained more of the game. He told me the rulers decapitated the sacrificial players using an obsidian blade, a symbolic action. Many ancient cultures thought demons became visible in polished obsidian, like scrying tools.

He got that look on his face. Difficult to describe, but a calmness washed over him, and his eyes grew soft.

He continued, "Modern man can't see the cosmology like the Olmec. For them, death acted as a mechanism for correct living. For us, it's all about safety. We're addicted to it. In the finale, the most common form of sacrifice was heart-extraction. They cut out their fucking hearts. The heart was the center of the individual and a fragment of the Sun's heat. They considered the Sun to be a heart-soul. In their view, humanity's divine 'sun fragments' were 'trapped' by the physical body and its desires. With the physical form disposed of, the divine nature was free. Fucking wild stuff."

For the rest of the evening, he expounded upon the idea by comparing it to Crowley's quote from *The Book of the Law*, "Every man and every woman is a star." While he spoke, I thought of living in such a dangerous place. The threat of death, the peril, it mutated me.

Perhaps when the city died, its soul became free.

II

EM

Detroit—the more the buildings slumped into themselves and the roads succumbed to grass, the more the city became an idea rather than a place. An abstraction that pulled certain minds into it to fill those holes and gaps. Ours were minds that could thrive in such a place.

Which is to say the city left you alone to think. It never intruded. Much like Ryan himself, who knew which question to ask as well as when to ask it, Detroit remained quiet while you talked out what was hidden deep inside.

Often it was a matter of juxtaposition. A copse of trees in an old parking lot, a vine crawling through a billboard. The city disrupted, and as it caught you looking, puzzling over how such a thing could come to pass, the beauty of it even, you caught yourself thinking. Surprised yourself before you even knew you were aware.

I never really thought about what Detroit must have been like before. It was beyond history, which was odd, since the past should have been the first question on my mind. But it wasn't. The city had slipped away from time unannounced. A fugitive place, cast off, exiled. It existed for itself. Perhaps that was the charm, its secret. It had given history the slip.

But not time. Curiously enough time was highlighted. By evading the past it became pure present. But with this difference—it became pure time as well. Etched on every eroded brick, a time both in motion and halted, simultaneously. As if photo and film had collided, leaving you wondering where to look.

CK

A dream came. I sat in a lawn chair next to a small bonfire in the backyard of my parents' suburban house. It was the late 1980s before I met Ryan. Regardless, there he stood, almost thirty-years old and motionless, staring straight ahead like a military man. An army of fire ants appeared near the bonfire pit. Ryan stared into space. Ants marched into the coals single file. Ryan remained silent as the fire didn't harm the ants. Breaking the silence, Ryan said something about being a "space cadet." The words haunted me. Something about the word "cadet" seemed serious despite the "spacey" connotations. Ants continued crawling around the fire unharmed. Ryan turned with his lopsided grin and said, "Gotta save the little guys."

Erik and I entered the city to merge with the fire, but the city fought against us. How does one integrate into a place filled with so much opposition?

CK

In Detroit, difficulties challenged one's mettle while one tried to function at a basic human level. From ratty liquor shops that doubled as grocery stores to the laundromats that acted as fronts for drug pushing, the city's infrastructure had crumbled to smithereens long ago. Trying to accomplish day-to-day matters became problematic. It messed with you, like the city had adopted a malicious sentience. As the difficulties piled up, Detroit seemed like a vengeful god who punished fools stupid enough to try and tame it.

One such punishment occurred with my truck. It went the way of the dodo after I hit a gargantuan winter pothole at 45 mph and broke the axle. I had to total the truck—too expensive to fix. This was after somebody broke the driver's side window. The thief stole a dozen compact discs and all the spare coins in the ashtray. Detroit was always gobbling up the things that might make life easier or more pleasurable.

After that, I cycled every week to the seedy laundromat, but that wasn't without its own misfortunes. In a city where most people didn't give a fuck, beer bottles and expletives got thrown around like fertilizer on farmland. I ran over broken glass and my front tire exploded. I lugged the bike and laundry a half mile back to my apartment cursing the whole way.

These struggles often coincided with messages from the universe hidden within synchronicity. Ryan remained curious about their secret correlations. Maybe I didn't need the truck. These struggles were the universe showing me I didn't need as much as I thought. As superfluities whittled away, I became more determined to simplify life. This directed attention acted as yoga, transforming my desire for convenience into Spartan living.

EM

City of rusted iron and crumbling concrete. Its decay fit us well. In it we found a clearing, a place to take stock, a chance to rebuild to suit our own tastes. Part of the allure was certainly the danger of such a place. Where anything could happen to anyone, at any time. But the freedom we all found there was a function of the architecture itself. A cleared field would have been too open, would have afforded too much space. Nothing to push against, nothing to grab and poach into a new beginning. And America's great cities, its established ones, its New Yorks, Chicagos, and San Franciscos would have been too already-there. Nowhere to move, no room to breathe. It was in this vacated city, this wasteland of debris and ramshackle and make-do, where one found a foothold and the materials with which to begin anew.

CK

The ruins were in constant reconfiguration. Street people lived below the train tracks in the Eastern Market. This acted as its own subterranean ecosystem. Other homeless people marked territory around the Greyhound Bus Station and the smaller bus stops around town. Squatters took over abandoned houses making them livable. Aggressive homeless people frequented the areas with whites because the urban neighborhoods didn't provide enough disposable cash. Some hung out downtown, but the cops patrolled this area more because of the Renaissance Center and Hart Plaza, the face of Detroit. One would run into a street person around the Fox Theater but police patrols put a stop to it because of the newly built Comerica Park. Urban spelunkers went into abandoned buildings, but I thought them foolish. They saw it as a romantic way to reconnect with the city but it was dangerous. Perhaps these people believed they were invincible. But one doesn't handle a snake if one doesn't want to get bit. For a long time, Detroit was America's murder capital, and it made little sense to put yourself in danger needlessly. They considered it a joy ride. The abandoned train station was their usual haunt, but they also frequented the train tracks under Eastern Market and derelict factories like the Fisher Body Plant 21 and the Packard Plant.

People cannibalized the skeletal remains of buildings and made them into something new. A forgotten warehouse might become an art gallery. A burned-out house might become an outreach center. A broken-down garage might turn into a hipster restaurant. The city shirked traditional building codes. A vibrant energy existed because anything could happen and anything rebuilt from the destruction made the city more unique. Miraculously, the city refused to die, but reinvented itself with urban farming or a housing collective. A friend even refurbished an abandoned funeral home into a huge living space where he paid his rent by having parties every month.

The city was beautiful, but one had to have the right perspective to see it. The Guardian Building had its Art Deco design. The Book Building was a masterpiece of Italian Renaissance–style. The Detroit Opera House in the Grand Circus Park Historic District, restored in 1996, was a marvel to behold. I had a part-time painting job helping with the last remnants of the restoration so it gave me the chance to see areas the public never saw. Places like the Boston Edison Historic district or Belle Isle were beautiful areas with wildlife and a calming effect. Greektown was a lively area with casinos and restaurants. The People Mover connected to the historic Joe Louis Arena, which was near Cobo Center, the place that held the North American International Auto Show.

Detroit's beauty rested in the juxtaposition of past and present. The decay fit well, a foil to the beautiful churches and architecture. These days people buy up houses and revitalize. Corporate brands invade areas comprising family-owned businesses. They erect ventures like Comerica Park and Ford Field in the name of Corporate America. Rents skyrocket and adventure moves on.

EM

Social life in Detroit took place in a series of oases, where weary travelers found respite from the wasted streets and lots and overgrown ruins that littered the spaces between.

One needed that safe camp. It didn't really matter the exact function of the edifice itself—bar, restaurant, an apartment building stranded on a block of wrecked houses. What mattered was the sanctuary one found inside. A modern caravanserai, where people strewn about the city mingled in the unstable truce of conspiracy. Welded together by necessity, by the lack of other such offerings, a crowd would gather in a camaraderie all the more intense because fleeting. Everyone knew that, sooner rather than later, doors would close and they would be thrust out into the cold, into the twisted iron and rotted wood, into the dead-weeded back lots beginning to fill with drifted snow. At night it was always a long walk home.

EM

A white person walking down the street drew attention. A white person on the bus drew second glances.

You never could disguise race of course but it was best to conceal it. In winter it was easier; it hid under a frayed coat or in a hoodie. Always walk to the middle of the bus. Too close to the driver and you looked scared, but too far back invited inquiry. Though you could never escape that.

"Hey White Boy!"

I sunk even deeper into my seat, huddled against the glass. Sometimes they went away after a few tries.

"Hey White Boy!"

The voice was moving closer, seat by seat. I could feel it encroach.

"Yo White Boy!"

There was no escape now. To answer immediately invited disdain, and gave off a message of weakness. But to completely ignore it showed it bothered you. And that was unacceptable. Or worse, it was mistaken for fear.

"White Boy..."

He was right behind me now. I would have to respond. But he would have to earn it first. A few more and the other passengers would recognize it for the harassment it was. Or so I hoped.

"Yo man why wouldn't you answer?"

"I'm not a boy."

"Hey man you got a cigarette?"

"I don't smoke."

"Alright."

Was I learning to abide, or to withdraw into myself? The answer was never clear.

CK

Every weekend the suburbanites came down for a sporting event or concert. Urbanites hated these times because the bourgeoisie didn't live there, so why should the outsiders partake in the city's events without contributing? The survivors roughed it out day to day, and they didn't like tourists.

The old-timers, the 60s holdouts, were rare individuals. They were like unicorns. Occasionally, they'd stride out of their forsaken neighborhoods and make their presence known. They had a matter-of-factness about them. I'm not surprised because living and struggling in that mess for thirty or forty years seems laughable. One had to respect their resilience. Easily identified, they carried a somber, hard quality. My regular taxi driver was one. I'm sure he had seen crazy shit in his day. I knew a few bartenders like this. They eyed people who came down for the games like, "How DARE YOU come to MY city."

All the African Americans living in the various neighborhoods had their opinions about us. They ranged from curious to supportive, to tolerant, to indifferent, to disdainful, to hostile. I seldom met Black people who didn't treat me like an outsider, like I didn't belong. I don't blame them. Whites left the city to rot.

CK

When my bike became operational, I rode it to work through the darker areas off Russell, amid the no-man's-land between Hamtramck and New Center, a place nobody would venture through at night because of too many abandoned factories and few working lights. It became an adventure swerving around trash and potholes. Each time, I passed an underworld of filth where homeless people gathered in their own ecology. Warming their hands around oil-drum fires, the broken men seemed like night terrors or future possibilities of what I might become if I didn't try harder to survive. The flames made their silhouettes look like demons ready to devour. As I whizzed by pedaling as fast as possible, hurrying to get to a more civilized area of the city, they yelled at me.

These shouts in my direction became routine whenever I commuted via bike, foot, or bus. As a white man in a Black city, anger at our class division was palpable. Then again, anyone who spent more than a few minutes downtown realized their calls were justified. As you journeyed on with your attention focused anywhere else but at the people passing, white guilt made you feel terrible for not giving the homeless people your entire paycheck. You'd wait for the inevitable: "Hey man, gotta dollar?"

Or... "Hey white boy, where ya going?"

Or... "I don't give a fuck!"

Ad nauseam.

EM

The Detroit criminal is a special breed. His transgression never feels personal; it's always "strictly business."

One of the several acts perpetrated against me while in Detroit was a break-in that occurred when I left for my parents' house in Minnesota. The thief entered through a window, ripping open the protective screen and knocking out a portion of the glass. He then proceeded to open it, stepping onto my desk which was against the wall. He took my video cassette player, some compact disks, and my leather jacket. This last item was particularly difficult to lose, since I had always wanted to own a leather jacket but always felt self-conscious about wearing one. Now that I had the nerve, it was gone. But what was curious about the incident was the way the thief treated three small ceramic figurines that Julie had given me for my birthday. One was of a giraffe, one was an elephant, and the other was a zebra, all meant to recall a pleasant day spent frolicking together at the zoo during a carefree moment of our relationship. I had put these figures on my desk to remind me of Julie, and the criminal must have broken them while stepping down onto my workspace from the window above. I found them later, placed back into their original shapes and laying one right next to the other, on the chair in the hall.

Did the thief fear the power that these charged objects might inflict? Did he experience a pang of remorse at breaking a personal object? Or was the message simply "Sorry, I didn't come for these pieces and did not mean to break them. I just needed money"?

EM

It's a funny thing being publicly accused. I'm not talking about getting a letter or a summons or being called out for a comment on the internet. I mean to actually physically stand before a crowd as everyone determines for themselves whether or not you're guilty.

It happened to me at a Detroit bus stop. I was waiting for the bus, minding my own business. A sizeable crowd gathered. Then this homeless guy started talking to me. I'd seen him before and knew he was a bit crazy. I remembered him distinctly because of the strange way he would become more and more aggressive as time went on. The range of his behavior was startling.

They'd let him out of a halfway house or jail cell and at first he'd even be pretty tame. You could tell he'd just been released because of the docile way he would act. It was creepy. He came on like an adult child, mumbling and shuffling his feet, looking down and even talking in a child's voice. But then the child in him grew up. He got more confident, then more aggressive, and soon his under-the-breath mumbling became outright threat. I had even seen him knock over a woman. The cops came and handcuffed him, restarting his life's cycle.

So when I saw him at the bus stop I immediately wondered at what stage he was at. Despite my best efforts to avoid his glance, or perhaps because of it, he began talking with me, and soon enough I had my answer. With nowhere for me to go, just hoping the damn bus would finally come, he announced to the crowd: "I remember you, you were that white guy that raped that little Black girl." I was simultaneously flabbergasted, appalled, and scared shitless. I quickly backed away, and scanned the faces of my all-Black jury. Luckily, my accuser did not strike the most trustworthy pose. I could see, in a moment of thankfulness, everyone trying to look away. White Guy was no child rapist—he had been found innocent. Just a poor white bastard who got called out by the crazy man at the bus stop in front of the Detroit Institute of Arts.

EM

As much as we loved Detroit, loved its challenges and its people, we were interlopers. This point was brought home to me one night at Baker's Keyboard Lounge. Billed as "the oldest jazz club in America," Baker's sits right on 8 Mile. It was one of the few places that I knew better than Ryan. I took him there one night to hear some jazz. The band, as usual, was amazing. It was the sort of place where musicians would sit by the stage, sipping a drink, waiting to be invited up to play with the band. For one number, a woman came up to perform vocals. She was outstanding, and as the band slowed down behind her, she began to tell a story. It was about how her man would invite his friends over, which the woman accepted, but how at times she would also want to be left alone with him in their house, enjoying their relationship separately. It was a nice interlude, and the all-Black crowd in the small, intimate club enjoyed it. But I couldn't help feeling that she was speaking to Ryan and me, the two guests that, while being accepted, should remember not to overstay their welcome in someone else's home.

EM

A hooker in a fur-collared coat hailed me with a welcoming smile as I rode my bike down a forlorn winter street. How could anyone be a failure in a city that failed? There was nothing left to lose.

The trick was to never show weakness. You were always being tested—at the bus stop, in the store, walking down the street—and your responses keenly judged. To appear fawning, unsure of oneself, or simply scared invited a guilty verdict. Being someplace you didn't belong was the ultimate crime in Detroit. But at the same time an outward show of force could quickly lead to violence. You had to send a message of respect, while at the same time letting everyone know that you would only accept so much before pushing back. Life in Detroit seemed to exist on this razor's edge separating meek and strong. Detroit didn't reward nakedness. It thought it naive. Giving yourself up to it completely was tantamount to making yourself a victim—and being treated accordingly.

The city could eat you up, and it did precisely that to quite a few people. But for others who could withstand the bite, it was like a shot in the arm, an inoculation against all that you knew or assumed. The ultimate test was against the city, and the deeper you went the more you could potentially reap . . . or lose. In that gamble you could discover who you really were. That was the allure of Detroit.

CK

The city was knee-deep in drugs. The narcotic of choice depended on one's station in life and one's trajectory. Were you going up or down? Syringes and broken crack pipes on the sidewalks were a common sight. Club kids who got in too deep became the most tragic instances. A young woman I knew started doing ecstasy at raves and ended up losing everything because crack got her. It was her boyfriend's fault. He was a DJ, so he had the hook-ups. Waiting at the bus stop you'd see a guy wrapped in ratty clothes rocking back and forth in need of a fix. A hipster at the back of the Bronx Bar waiting for his pusher. A bar's bathroom door closed and the sound of sniffing and giggling. These were the signs.

People knew Detroit for its rock n' roll scene. Performing in front of a crowd isn't easy, and I had many friends and acquaintances who did a line or ten before a show. A few got hooked on heroin and they ruined their budding careers because they didn't respect the beast and the monkey took them down a deep, dark hole. Same with people in the kitchens around town. Dishwashers would nod off. Cooks were high as a kite. Bartenders needed speed to get through the long hours. It's lucky I got out of there without a major addiction (unless you count alcohol, the accepted drug). I tried lots of things, but I was always drawn to psychedelics.

One time, at the Fourth Street Fair, Ryan hooked up with some thug types. I saw him chatting. He came back and told me we could get mushrooms but we needed $200. It was a lot of money. He said it was a big score and we could all have many doses. I hadn't shed all of my suburban fear and these guys looked rough. After I reluctantly agreed, Ryan mentioned we had to meet them in the McDonald's parking lot off the freeway. I got more frightened. I didn't know this would be an "official" drug deal; not just a passing of product in a crowd. My first thought was, "What if it's a set-up?"

We met two carloads in the lot and it terrified me—about four or five to a car. They made Ryan and I get in one car's back seat. They knew we were green. I don't know why we agreed to go in the back. Now I probably wouldn't have done that, but I trusted Ryan's intuition and he seemed okay with it. They gave us the bag. He inspected it and nodded. We gave them the money. As we exited, one guy said, "Yo man. It's safer on the other side. Best stay there."

Too bad we didn't have that advice sooner. The mushrooms were fakes.

CK

Detroit provided lots of inspiration so it became the perfect place for artists, writers, and musicians. It didn't matter that we braved the city. What mattered came from it. What did we create because of it? How did we recreate ourselves? How did the city shape us?

When Ryan examined my art or writing, he was present one-hundred percent. He maintained focus and presence. I loved him for that. He saw deeper than most people. After he left my life, I spent four years in art college with hundreds of people critiquing my work. In all that time, all those people never saw it, or never understood. They made comments about the compositions or ideas, but they never saw the magical revelation lurking inside. Ryan was the only person who saw. I assume his dabbling with psychedelics and meditation made this possible, or maybe he had a knack for recognizing subtlety. Most times, he spotted a psychological underpinning, a hidden message my inner self was trying to express. Art is the residue of an internal journey, the unraveling of the paradox between the conscious mind (the ego) and the unconscious mind, and Ryan translated its language.

He got excited whenever I made things—collages, paintings, writings, poetry, food, whatever. Those times he assessed my art were tough moments. Because of my artistic focus, I knew more about the rules and principles of design, but when he assessed my work I felt strange, like he was searching for something outside these perimeters, something more elusive, a spawning of the mysterious like algae in a pond. He never explained in words, but his eyes conveyed the capture. He saw it. Then I saw it. We knew.

Because of yoga, his outlook on creation was Eastern—the act of making an object feeds the soul. Like Japanese calligraphy, the mark isn't important. The action defines immortality. Discussions about form or composition never happened. Design elements and principles remained unnecessary. Yes, he understood the basics we judge beauty upon; he knew more about art history and design than most people. However, his main concern was that I desired to create, that I made for the sake of making. He got excited by transcendence and the illusory nature of past and future, in favor of spontaneous ritual in the present. Evidence existed; there's no doubt. I painted to show. But he didn't care if I painted the Mona Lisa and later burned it. He fed off of that experience too because of its detachment. He was unsure of himself as a writer, but more because the result didn't matter to him. He didn't seem to want to publish. He didn't want fame. The experiential lesson writing provided was important to him. Write, then put it in a drawer. As both an artist and psychonaut, he inspired me to create with ferocity, bravely taking risks so my work could reflect the mystery within. Not just making art as decoration to enrich life, but to dig deeper into what makes one tick, and in turn, to understand reality on many levels, to dig into layers of psychology and to see how this influences synchronicity in the outer world. By harnessing the inner self, one could see the outer world more clearly. The microcosm affects the macrocosm. I reflected the universe on a different scale, but that same mystery that baffles progress lived inside me. Making art with this in mind was an expedition into the deep universe within and I brought back artifacts of consciousness from those sacred spaces above and below. This is what he encouraged: confronting the unknown, diving into the murkiness of the psychological shadow.

We became so in-tune with our art and writing we fed off each other in surprising but sometimes dangerous ways. When I dove deep into my subconscious I dredged up disturbing ideas that manifested as collaged monstrosities— nightmarish images pasted together from pornography, children's coloring books, and animal magazines. These images were the most unequivocally raw work I've ever done. With each one, he pushed me further. The work became more potent. His push wasn't influence—more like facilitation. That's what he did with people. His faith in my artistry allowed me to search for myself in those darker areas. Art shouldn't be a pretty picture. Art should make one fall down a deep well. Each trip down provided a boon.

EM

Ryan was more writer than visual artist but one piece that always stuck with me was his curious projection art of Hansel

and Gretel. A slide of the fairy tale siblings, surrounded by a
forest motif, was projected onto a wall almost every time I
was at his suburban apartment. The effect was eye catching.
The forlorn pair wandered a stylized forest searching for
their way back. But what really arrested my attention was
trying to figure out why he had chosen Hansel and Gretel.
It was by no means the obvious choice. At first I thought
it had to do with the idea of "the search" itself. But the two
waifs are always looking backwards, trying to return. Was
he trying to return somewhere, and if so, where? Given his
interest in magic, I also thought maybe it had to do with
the Witch, the defeat of the evil crone as a metaphor for
overcoming a problem, dilemma, or issue. But he never
seemed to side with the common interpretation of "evil" in
popular imagination. It would have been more in keeping
for him to celebrate the Witch, much as he sympathized
with the Devil. Perhaps the fairy tale encapsulated the way
he thought about the city. Him and his girlfriend cast adrift
in the dark urban forest that is Detroit, lost, breadcrumbs
nibbled away by the city's hungry denizens, enticed by the
house of sugar that is ultimately a trap. But what is so sweet
about Detroit? Maybe it was his outlook on the whole world,
a too-sweet confection that only serves to fatten one up for
the pot. He wanted to shove that old Witch into the oven.

Ryan saw himself as a writer, but he kept his work hidden
in a box under his bed. I only saw that box once. He gave so
much away but then again he could be so secretive, perhaps
in order to keep something for himself. Or from fear. A
deep-seated fear that he never let out. How could someone
that strong, that fearless, be at the same time hesitant and
unsure? Perhaps he was an artisan of the spoken word, of
the gesture, the voice. He convinced by his presence. It was

more than simply the validation of his utterances. It was part and parcel to them, simultaneous and equal. You could easier separate flour from bread than his speech from his being.

He was more of a life artist than anything else. He wrote, sure, and became interested in a number of projects in several media. But in the end, his life was his art, his way of being his canvas. It would have been easy for him to sell the old Romantic line of Art (with capital A) as a creation of the troubled artist. The lie of the genius. His genius was discovering that we're all geniuses. I was the lone academic, the non-Artist, but through him discovered that the cooking I did, the walks I took through the city, even the scholarly prose I wrote, was also Art when done with a certain state of mind.

CK

One night, I took the bus to his apartment in the suburbs to make Art together. He treated psychology as a tool and the mind a canvas, but I never saw him paint.

Whenever an artist begins a work, a moment of resistance ensues associated with that first step toward fear. Steven Pressfield's book *The War of Art* discusses how terrifying it is to work through this fear. In most other endeavors Ryan acted without pause, but this time I saw him afraid. His girlfriend Mandy, a sculptor and Thelemite, lurked about sneaking peeks at our blank pieces of cardboard. Her presence made us nervous.

After several minutes, we began. Painting in a flurry of movements, we finished the portraits in less time than it took to gather the courage to create them. When I saw his painting it stunned me. It was superb. Better than I imagined. Childlike in execution and filled with electrified color, it sang. Somehow, he sidestepped the conventions of painting a portrait that resembled me, or even resembled a person. Instead, he made something that expressed my essence. An abstraction with intricacies, deep psychological facets I didn't know existed within myself. He found something inside, an invisible quality. Later this quality became visible. However, when he illustrated it, it seemed like a characteristic only he could see. Like most of his other endeavors, this artwork enchanted those who saw it—a magic mined out of presence, an energy.

I also surprised him with my portrayal. I covered the cardboard in intense oranges, greens, and yellows. It appeared like I skinned him and a strange energy lurked beneath. It reminded me of Clive Barker's Cenobites. He flipped his lid when he saw it. He often got excited by art, but this time was different. His excitement came from our captured essences, seen through the illusion of flesh, realizing body remains a clever way to hide soul.

EM

I often wondered what Ryan took from me. He connected mainly with artists, not academics. He was most at home with creative types, those who pushed the boundaries of the imagination. He also spent a lot of time working with the mentally ill, who often drained his energy as he attempted to guide them out of their labyrinths. Of course, he could fit into most situations, find some type of common ground with most anybody, and it was only mildly surprising that he ended up working as a telemarketer. But why me? I was interested in literature, it was true, but with an analytic rather than artistic gaze. I remember one time he told me, "You, I'm not sure what you are." It made me proud somehow, and a bit worried—I didn't know the answer either. Perhaps it was the mystery of an academic seeking the path that attracted him. He was so used to his disciples coming from a place of irrationality, that to see a more rational thinker searching for the same sort of truths as he did must have challenged his assumptions about what the path was all about. And he loved a challenge.

CK

Ryan drove around looking for eccentrics to help. Stopping at the random coffee shop. A department store. A prison. Giving feedback. On to the next one. Back to the vehicle. Too many people to see tonight. Too many seekers in need of revelation.

His friends were exotic dancers, hotheaded accountants, war veterans, fringe intellectuals, misunderstood mystics, street people, outsider artists, and drug addicts. To him, these misfits became opportunities to encourage growth, to inspire becoming, to shape visionaries. Sometimes, he accomplished what he set out to do. More times than not, people balked at what he offered. Making concepts like chaos, ego obliteration, sex magic, and Kali desirable wasn't easy, but give him credit for trying.

He wasn't fussy about his friends per se. Many people choose the like-minded as friends, but that wasn't him. Ryan watched people evolve, saw how they shirked the mold. He relished the differences. Dissolving the veil that blocked an individual from understanding their true nature became his greatest pleasure. He loved to find people who struggled with psychological rock bottom, amid an identity crisis as they verged on self-discovery.

Ryan invested everything into these eccentrics. He often showed up at an event or party with one in tow. Somebody he met in a late-night diner, or a downtown gas station convenience store in the morning's early hours. A veteran from the Iraq War who worshiped Kali. A female Thelemite he met at a rock show who became a "fuck buddy" but not a girlfriend. A stripper he brought over to my house once to annoy my ex-wife Gayle. Many people from many walks of life. A sleep researcher. A man named after a Romantic poet who became a heroin addict. A reclusive guy who had a thousand keyboards but never played music on them. An accountant who used Thelemic magic to make a shit-ton of money. An academic who took part in an ecstasy study. A prude who transformed into a burlesque artist. An intellectual who turned into a psychedelic drug advocate. A dejected homemaker who became a sexual mystic. Many kinds of people, all sharing one trait—uniqueness.

Ryan embraced those with wider possibilities. He fed from those people. He loathed people who didn't have the courage to transform. If you couldn't risk psychological change, if you couldn't take that leap, he didn't give you the same energy. That's not to say he wouldn't try, but he knew enough about a transformative experience to discern who's ready and who's not. He demanded complete devotion to mutation. Many people tried and failed or just tagged along. He called them "tourists."

CK

Most of our conversations happened in automobiles, which seems like such a Detroit—and by extension,

American—thing to do. Each time, it was the same. He called me up at two in the morning. He said something like, "Come over. Now. I found it." What he found wasn't an epiphany or a nugget of wisdom. What he found was ongoing, a wavelength, a harmony, an intellectual link between us. Inside this connection, we talked for hours about all topics with few restrictions. One night, it was the new John Zorn album and its manic jazz riffs. Next, it was the risqué photography of Sally Mann and her bravery as a creator. Then a startling revelation about Henry Darger that evening. His arms flew up in the air. His energy became manic. Each time, we resumed the ongoing conversation that started at that crazy movie theater as teenagers. It's possible we maintained one conversation, and it lasted decades, perhaps lifetimes, getting interrupted by mundane things like eating, working, and sleeping. When these talks occurred, the energy became palpable. Insomnia took hold. Our exchange of energy wired me. Our meetings at coffeehouses and diners became like trips to church. He adored these late-night places nearly as much as the bewildered souls he found lingering in them. These places acted as Purgatorio and he was the Virgil who guided the Damned out of darkness. And the night was his element. Down empty streets, he drove around in an endless search. His destination was a Ram's Horn restaurant or a Denny's in the suburbs, or Lafayette Coney Island or The Clock Restaurant downtown. I'm not sure of his range, but I imagine him traveling several miles from one end of the city to the other, just to find that one seeker. That one he missed. That one who might be hiding. He knew everyone in these places: the single-mom waitresses looking for an affair, the ex-con cooks looking for redemption, the college kids looking for psychedelic experience, the armchair philosophers looking for a sparring partner, the perverts looking for understanding, all of them. Sometimes at our meetings, he introduced me to a random person. Their friendships seemed impossible, but he didn't consider them friendships per se, more like projects. It made me wonder if I was a project too or actually his friend. These days I think I was both. While we talked, he often mentioned that he had a crazy conversation with these people months back about something or other. On some occasions, he said, "I had sex with them." And on even fewer occasions, he added, "Do you wanna join next time?"

CK

In our late-night meetings driving around aimlessly, he seemed to be eluding capture by an unknown pursuer. Perhaps the FBI or CIA tailed him. He was paranoid. I didn't know if a real threat existed or if it was an acid flashback. His paranoia invaded his social life too. He thought people stole his ideas, so he kept his writing hidden away. On rare occasions he showed random thoughts. One time, he let me read a piece about Jonah and the Whale inside a black hole written with an experimental structure. It was a bizarre tale, if you could call it a story at all. He lost his patience with me for not understanding what he tried to convey. This confused reaction caused him to retreat, at least with me.

A few years later, I experimented with writing folklore. His impression was that I stole his idea even though my myth didn't have Jonah, whales, or black holes. The premise of time and space crashing down might have inspired me. But he seemed overly sensitive. How could these ideas not inspire you? Awakening. Mutation. Transcendence. How could someone with so many ideas not influence you?

Everyone knew he was working on a magnum opus but he seldom showed us anything. Perhaps he was insecure. Perhaps he didn't trust me. Maybe he wasn't writing at all. I'm not sure. His work was probably too extreme, perhaps even illegal, but this remains speculation on my part. Maybe he felt I wouldn't understand, or at the very least, judge him for his crimes.

In many ways, I felt pity for him. Sometimes, people troubled him. But his frustration came from his own inability to articulate his thoughts. His writing might have succeeded, but one can't write one's way out of a social interaction. Especially when one is trying to explain complex metaphysical ideas to people who don't want to be challenged. Ryan revealed these concepts to me in riddles, sometimes in writing and sometimes verbally. Maybe speaking of these mysteries remains impossible. Maybe his frustration and paranoia stems from this. What if he told the wrong person? What if they misinterpreted it? What if I did?

EM

"I probably shouldn't show you this." And he was right—he shouldn't have. But he did. In his black Saturn, in a late-night parking lot, in a cold but snowless November, he slid the burned disk into its player. Modest Mouse's *The Lonesome Crowded West*. Those looped lyrics that lamented a new America of strip malls and corporate homogenization grabbed me, and pulled me under with them.

Ryan had a knack for introducing the right album, book, or idea to the right person. Usually just when they needed it most. He was the first to introduce me to the work of the theorists Gilles Deleuze and Félix Guattari. We spent hours talking about their ideas, which went on to inform our thinking and my first book. His interests were wide-ranging, and even when some of the works he offered didn't prove fruitful for me I was always grateful to encounter them. I never could penetrate much of the magical texts, but the Vedic literature he lent me reverberated. You never knew what he was going to come up with but it was always thought-provoking.

Influence went both ways. I introduced him to Samuel L. Delany's strange novel *Dahlgren*, whose rendition of a magical burned-out city resonated with my Detroit experience. And I responded to his love of Kenneth Anger with a slew of avant-garde and underground films. Part of his attraction was the stimulation he brought in terms of new ideas, texts, and concepts. But as our relationship intensified it became harder and harder to disentangle my thoughts and interests from his, and our talks became a nexus of readings, previous discussions, and shared ideas that would continue from where we left off the meeting before. It was an intoxicating time for me, and the things we discussed still influence me, even after the years have gone by.

CK

Ryan fought against a spiritually deficient society, and it exhausted him. That's why he eventually became a hermit. Like a dragon retreating to a cave, we didn't see him for months. Then he woke, brushed off his wings, left the self-imposed exile to initiate new mutants. Urbanite or suburbanite? It didn't matter to him, but flexibility did.

Obstinate people troubled him; those who didn't budge on their indoctrination. These people bought the illusion, so they developed fabrications to conform. Indoctrination crushed their authenticity, that inner spark he looked for, by obliterating what he called the "child." He hated that emptiness. Barren people reinforcing the lies told to them, perpetuating the program he despised. Conformists often challenged his patience. He didn't have time to deal with them. Too far gone to mutate. Not close enough to the edge. Usually, these people spotted him in a crowd and went after him. Ryan might call them out, so they acted quickly and fiercely. Deliver the first strike. Stir up the bile. Spit venom.

He became ruthless when necessary, but he was also merciful when someone was at a psychological low. He would often appear suddenly to those going through a spiritual crisis, those who were going through Jungian individuation. To these people, he was a savior. But to those he deemed weak, to those who weren't malleable, he could be merciless. His eyes could change suddenly. In a single conversation, they might shine with a prophet's love and then burn with a zealot's cruelty. People often hated him for the changes individuation thrust upon them. If they weren't ready, he seemed diabolical, malevolent, crazy, manipulative, whatever. But that was false. He might be the world's most valuable type of person, certainly the sanest. That became the irony. Society needs more people like him, but fear kept people from him.

CK

Ryan had kinship with a man named Bobby Soul. Clad in diabolical black, Bobby was a dark man with darker motivations. When Ryan introduced us at Detroit's most popular street fair, the Dally in the Alley, Bobby stared through me. He was a black hole with a formidable aura, and when we made eye-contact, his witchery pulled me in his direction. Two beautiful women on his arms, those runaway Susan Atkins types, proved he didn't play by the rules.

It was possible to be friends with Ryan because we found common ground. When Ryan spoke of magic, people often thought of voodoo and human sacrifice. Superstition is a powerful belief, and it was interesting to see how far assumptions were from the real man. Yes, Ryan was quite intimidating when he wore his devilish mask, but he could also don the benevolent mask of a teacher. Bobby was just unsettling. Bobby had no mask. He was an unscrupulous character who did questionable things. That was obvious. He represented the city's dark side. He was the real deal, a wizard, and he lived in Detroit because it gave him the anonymity that a larger, functioning city couldn't allow. Bobby was like one of Lovecraft's doomed heroes who saw too much of the universe's madness. That look of deep, bottomless void rested in his empty eyes.

I never knew much about Bobby. Ryan's praises told me what I needed to know. Ryan looked up to him. It was obvious by the reverence he showed. For Ryan to look up to the man, this guy had to have something exceptional about him.

A few years after Ryan exited my life, I dove deep into occult practices. I read. I studied. I meditated. I practiced. I performed. I went deeper into the occult mystery and I found dark things there. I touched something in that pool that rested in Bobby's eyes. A haunting within life. I understand him now because I delved deeper into the shadows of the occult world. I've taken on part of that same darkness. Innocence transforms into experience, and the older we get, the more we take on our true selves, the more we unravel the mystery of our becoming.

EM

Bobby Soul couldn't have been his real name. I have vague memories of meeting him, but that yearly festival that took place behind my house, Dally in the Alley, was always filled with vague memories. Like the time I bought a Burroughs adding machine there in the early afternoon for 20 bucks. It was a peculiar festival, located behind the buildings, in the trash-strewn alleyways where sumac trees shot their trunks through broken concrete and birds sifted through the trashcans. Everyone was welcome, and everyone came, starting in the sunlit afternoon hours with casual beer and browsing for knickknacks before proceeding to twilight and the more serious debauches night brought. Anything was possible, even a man named Bobby Soul. The memory I do have involves a circle of sycophants surrounding him, enclosing their guru. If there was indeed such a man named Bobby Soul in the middle of that throng, a Sun possessed of such powers, Ryan would certainly have been the dowser's wand that would have witched him up. Ryan had a sort of sixth sense for such encounters. He was attuned. I have memories, vague memories of watching him enter any number of conversations, and becoming immediately involved, as if meeting a long-lost friend. But Bobby Soul, aptly named, was someone Ryan mentioned occasionally, a leader even for him. It was curious to see Ryan speak to him. He was not in the circle; he remained distinct from Bobby Soul's other "followers." But Ryan clearly respected him, and even acted deferential, which was a rare sight. So what did Ryan learn from him? What might he have taken from Ryan? Those answers are beyond my ken. But I do know this: I wanted to become a star, not orbit one.

CK

Despite his vague relationship with Bobby Soul, Ryan was the only person I ever met who lived without a ruler—an anarchist in every way, self-governed. We all have people who rule us. Some let the academic system rule them, but he rejected that in favor of intellectual freedom. Some let our jobs rule, but his jobs became a means to an end, not a career. Some let spouses rule, but he preferred open relationships. He envisioned a world without rulers, a society free of attachment and control. Most people deify politicians. He didn't trust them, calling them black magicians. Most people bow to entertainment. He saw it as indoctrination. Even magic was a symbiosis, not a subserviency.

Ryan donned different masks for different people, but he was an anarchist in its purest form. Not like punk bands or the style. The Sex Pistols weren't true anarchists because producer-created boy-bands can't be anarchy. Clothes don't make the anarchist. Neither do styles nor trends. He didn't have a style like them. He was too bookish to be cool, but he exuded coolness anyway because he didn't care about image.

In a more Taoist approach, a "pathless way," he was truly anarchist. He wasn't a nihilist either. He didn't "Rage Against the Machine." Ryan wanted to move through the machine with perception. He wanted to rework the cogs, one by one. It's better to weave through a construct than to tear it down because what will replace it? Understanding that the construct held little power over him conferred true freedom. Ryan became one of the few who trusted the universe enough to allow himself to flow with that current.

Detroit's anarchist/punk scene, in the Garden Bowl, Todd's on 7 Mile, and the Trumbullplex, thrived but most of these people hated Ryan. He became the true subversive because he remained a chameleon. He didn't need liberty spikes, piercings, or a Black Flag patch to prove his point. He traveled anywhere and did anything without people giving him a second glance and that was his true power. He performed magic on those who remained unaware of his influence. An undercover therapist of sorts, he wanted to break the persona and reveal the self. He wanted us to remove the masks we wear to convince us we're not monsters. "I'm this" and "you're that" never entered Ryan's head.

Sometimes he took on the air of an intellectual. Other times he lashed out against the intellectuals saying they were "tools of the system." He blasted The Melvins or The Michael Yonkers Band while moshing in the pit, but then he consoled a heartbroken suburban runaway. He saw through the punk disguise, but he'd still help if he could. Probably more than they realized. To him, they hid behind the costume because of fear of self. All the people who picked a side, who picked a group to feel more comfortable, were his enemies, at least while they remained in that frozen position. If they broke free, he'd be right there.

He played a game with persona. He knew it became useful to adopt masks to get the job done, but that's all it was—a disguise. He intended to turn people on, so this subterfuge became worthwhile. People never knew what hit them when he broke character to reveal his true face. It must have been like Lon Chaney from *The Phantom of the Opera* unmasking—quite a shock, but a necessary reveal. The Man of a Thousand Faces. It's like he used the mask as a way in, as a seduction. Maybe the mask presented a lifeline, and I never saw his true face. Like if he revealed it, madness might take me, so he was sparing me that demon. Maybe what dwelled beneath his exterior was too terrible and beautiful for most people to understand, like Nietzsche's "All great things must first wear terrifying and monstrous masks..."

EM

Ryan could be funny, and he could be inadvertently funny. Sometimes the two collided, and when they did, a subtle type of self-reflexive humor emerged. At those times he would catch the ridiculousness of his own position and laugh. I often think that those moments might have been the most revealing. Certainly to see him smile, to laugh at his own oddities and contradictions was revealing. These were usually moments of contradiction, when he caught himself preaching one thing but practicing another. Then he opened up another side of himself, and you felt you really knew him; you felt closer.

Otherwise, he wasn't what you would traditionally call funny. Certainly not a joker, or prankster. He was generally much too serious for that. Not like he couldn't tell or share a joke. More like his natural demeanor didn't run to the comedic. And when he was funny in the traditional sense it was more of a byproduct. We all shared a mutual friend named Drew. A great guy really—we all liked him. But an antithesis to Ryan's teachings, an anti-Ryan. So Ryan takes to calling him "Drewcifer." He most likely began it seriously, or half-seriously, but the main thing was it caught the kernel of truth in a funny way—Drew was interested in a world of distraction, of gadgetry and games. But when I first heard the phrase, I almost split my sides, it was so apt and so comical. We all laughed. When this occurred in front of Ryan I noticed an important distinction—he laughed, but less. For him the term was perfectly cast in terms of a description, not a joke. The humor was incidental.

CK

Whether serious or funny, his focus was always on the moment.

One night early in our friendship, he revealed the mystery of energy. We sat in his parents' garage after a few beers—atypical people enjoying a typical American pastime. His back faced the open garage door. To his left sat his girlfriend, Mandy. To his right sat my cousin. I sat across from Ryan. Our seating was important to him. He was adamant about these positions. Before we started, he said, "Consciousness is a round table." I got the feeling he wasn't referring to furniture. It was something else. Questions ran through my head. A plane? A psychic structure? An alternate reality? I wasn't sure. Years later, I understood after studying the occult, but it seemed like gibberish at the time. Earlier, he claimed he could move energy with his mind. We were skeptical kids with little experience in the occult.

He gave us instructions.

"Clear your minds," he whispered.

He paused. Then he added, "Close your eyes and grasp each other's hands. Like a chain. We're a chain now. They can't break us."

We did as he said. It felt a little ridiculous, but I was open-minded enough to give him the benefit of the doubt.

He continued by saying, "Imagine a ball of white light. Visualize the energy moving in your body. See it in your mind's eye."

We did so. After several seconds of visualization, he whispered, "Move the ball of energy to the person on your left."

After several moments of anticipation, I felt a slight tingle.

Without warning, energy moved through me. Opening my eyes to see if the others were feeling it confirmed my suspicions. This was real. We were moving energy with only our thoughts.

He continued directing us. Many times, energy moved through the circle. Round and round it moved. As it gained momentum, I felt something surging up from the center of my body. After several minutes, he said, "Okay, that's enough. I think you get it. We don't want to overdo it."

We let go. The experiment ended. We exchanged experiences. Miraculously, we all basked in a runner's high without moving a single muscle, endorphins flowed through our bodies. We created energy, moved it around between us, and the results were euphoric. It was unbelievable.

The experience was a turning point in my life. It was the first time I accepted his metaphysical claims as truth, and I realized the power of attention and meditation. We performed a magical experiment and felt actual results. He changed us that night. My cousin became a masseur using that energy to heal people. Mandy finished her degree in dream psychology and then became a nurse. I became an artist and bookmaker, and I later used this technique to practice Qabalah, Qi Gong, and Chaos Magic. He helped us understand that energy and consciousness persist and are interconnected with flesh in the moment.

CK

I truly believe Ryan found his Holy Guardian Angel. Like Honoré de Balzac's centenarian, it helped him achieve a certain immortal moment, creating a communication with his eternal soul. Ryan didn't fit his age, and I bet even now, almost twenty years later, he looks the same, and twenty years from now, he probably won't have aged much. Something about him haunted me, something ancient and all-knowing. Sometimes he related historical occurrences in confidence, as if he channeled them or experienced them firsthand. It sounds impossible, but it's true. I was skeptical that he somehow transcended death, but that was before I tuned into his wavelength, that was before I knew things about Crowley. In hindsight, he may have been living in many concurrent times and lives, at least through his meditations. This explained his focus on synchronicity and the ability to foresee events. Through yoga, he detached his soul from this moment, moved himself out of the present, so he could see all moments through the eyes of his Holy Guardian Angel. By focusing on the present (something he advocated) one might transcend it and see reality from a bird's-eye view. Like a tree, the immortal soul sheds leaves and these leaves act as our lives. The leaves fall but the tree remains. Perhaps, he might even be the reincarnation of Crowley. That would explain his connection to Detroit (Crowley spent about a year there in 1919), and his fascination with both Crowley's house and the Detroit Masonic Temple, the largest Masonic building in the world.

EM

Ryan certainly projected an air of knowing beyond his boyish face. You saw it in his eyes—a compassion born of a long-suffered understanding. As if he'd been here since the beginning and could understand exactly how you had arrived at an impasse or a consternation. Yet too he seemed curiously contemporary, up-to-date. He reconciled both tendencies. If he was immortal, it was a fresh immortality unwearied by previous travail. If a newborn babe in each present, then uncannily prescient and wise beyond his years. Always present and aware, always watching, always on-call.

CK

If I had been subservient enough to be his student, he wouldn't have wanted to teach me. He guided me because of my rebellious nature. He wanted his protégés to question everything. He was a teacher without teachings. A Zen master without Zen. He wanted me to see my contradictions and the illusions society created to yoke me, to see the enigma of existence. His directives revealed a way to see through illusions by delving deeper into oneself to mine inner gold, to gain power. Authenticity was the result, a truth-based power used to walk through the world fully aware. That was his endgame; a revolutionary act more potent and everlasting than political marching, planting a bomb, or completing a suicide mission. His purpose will endure because it was mercurial. His influence still resonates within me, mutates my consciousness, so I've been able to touch people similarly—the cure to William S. Burroughs's "Word Virus." A tonic for propaganda. Pass it on to the next seeker. Free them so they can free others from enslavement, so they can ride chaos without fear. Freedom to explore consciousness, which should be the sovereign right of any individual, but modern society tries to limit this by outlawing or discrediting methods that tune awareness. But you can't stop a thought. And you can't stop a mind that understands the thought crimes that once enslaved it.

Evidence was important to him. Don't believe him because he said it. Do it. Do your own experiment. Be it. See the results. Draw conclusions. Being impassioned toward results destroys the experiment. Use your consciousness to unravel your own self, and then the lies perpetrated by society will dissolve. Truth will remain. This should happen in all areas of life. Spirituality. Relationships. The Work. One should be merciless with oneself. One should let go.

EM

Ryan was my spiritual guide. He would never have claimed to be leading me, and at the time, I would have cringed at the assertion that I was following him. Time, however, brings clarity. Although he undoubtedly learned from me, I grew immeasurably from the time I spent in his presence.

Ryan was a force, and drew others into his orbit. How did he get this power? Where did it come from? Most perceived it as a vibe or mojo or energy that he took or appropriated. But where did it come from?

Others could see how it emanated from within his very self. It wasn't a conjured parlor trick or false bravado. It was him, and in endless supply.

And if you understood that it was coming from within the next step was obvious—how do I pull something like that out of myself? Because you had to know, deep down, that it was already there in you too, or you were already lost. You would always remain a lesser planet orbiting the star, drawing its light, hoping to get closer to the source when in reality it was there all along, inside you.

EM

I struggle to capture the essence of his attraction in a word. "Attraction" is not even correct. "Power"? He had it, but unless you understood the term as a force emanating from within, a validation of what happened inside him rather than a means of convincing others, you are liable to miss the point. "Force" is too physical, "Personality" too weak. The problem is that all these terms attempt to posit an idea of influence held over, against, or onto others. The essence of his hold on us is located in his uncanny ability to draw forth the "Power," "Force," even "Personality" latent in ourselves. To "activate" all the already-latent possibilities we either never knew existed or, more probably, only vaguely sensed until his presence prompted us to call them forth into conscious recognition. A curious power, to foster the power in others. Such an act was both self-negating and self-fulfilling, since fostering the growth of another did not augment himself, yet proved his own self not only sufficient to invoke such a change, but unthreatened by the power so unleashed.

Not that he couldn't channel this into commerce. Another of his ironies was that he used his infinitely successful ability to convince others as a means of financial support. He earned a living as a telemarketer (and before that, a vacuum salesman), and one assumes he could have gone on to a successful personal speaker career. Or he could have become a stockbroker. But turning his gifts into cash tired him. You could see it when he came by after work. I always thought it was the fact of selling his intangible talents for something so petty as money. Perhaps that was true. But giving exhausted him, too. Later I found that he had to quit a job working at a mental health facility because of the psychic costs of sharing his gift, over and over. All the more joy, then, when I felt I was giving something back to him. Would that it had happened more often.

Where did it begin, his power? It was so easy to read it in his preoccupations. He was, as mentioned, the first to introduce me to yoga. And his Thelemite interests went back to his high school days. But it would be wrong to read these as providing a starting point. They fueled the flame, they didn't strike the flint. It must have existed before. The key to the practice was that this power was, to some degree, latent in everyone. So how did he discover it, and when? Through another like himself? Like we did in him? Or was he one of a rare breed capable of spontaneous self-actualization?

CK

Binaries were his special preoccupation. He wanted to synthesize opposites. He acknowledged the game board, black and white pieces, spaces, all the components, but he saw beyond them. Geometry and design. Chess and Go. Each half played its own game. Strategy. Systems. Polarized sides battling, but in need of synergy. He stepped outside the game board. Integrated opposites. Combined innocence and experience. Sublimated order and chaos. Action and inaction. Do without doing. Beyond good and evil. Beyond light and dark.

Ryan didn't come up with this himself. This synthesis exists all over history. In the esoteric symbolism of the Caduceus Wand, an emblem of Hermes that depicts two snakes winding around a winged staff. In the symbolism of the Baphomet character, an androgyny pointing "as above, so below." Jachin and Boaz, the light and dark pillars of Solomon's Temple. Yin and Yang. The lines and breaks of the I-Ching. He knew these symbols, these mandalas, and he mentioned their significance often. He knew the balanced individual needed both outlooks to be healthy; the West's emphasis on ego and action, the East's emphasis on nature and inaction.

Ryan was a serious scholar of Eastern mysticism, but not through any self-help bestseller way. This wasn't a game. This wasn't a fad or false ideology. No, he knew Western culture was sick. Sick to death. He knew he was sick because we're all sick. Across the board. Every one of us. Sick with the West's disposability and emphasis on money. Sick with Scientism. Sick with the idea we can choose religions and dispose of them when we tire of their significance and then move to the next religious skin. His search was anachronistic. He wanted out. He was tired of experts telling us what to do. Be your own expert, on everything. Hollowness is our place. Transcend it. With yoga, he was trying to balance the scales, rise above the game board. He was trying to be his own god, free from duality. Empty yet full.

EM

But his mind, too, had its partitions. The differentiation between East and West held his attention in particular, a dyad to which he would ceaselessly return. The East, in its myriad mystical forms, is oddly the easiest to depict. Bridging body and mind, the meditative fulcrum, that inner journey. It's what the West meant to him that's harder to pin down. The West, our own ocean we swam in, sometimes drowned in, was harder to see. What had it done for us? Ryan gave it its due as more than simply our oppressor, our blinder, our dead-hearted stepfather. And not just as that which goaded us on with the lash and the metal bit between our teeth. No, he realized the West had something to offer. A different sort of freedom. An opportunity to take off in a direction, in any direction, and never look back. To embrace suffering, court it, make something. To risk, wager, gamble. To build something new.

Little wonder he held Aleister Crowley, that great East-West synthesizer, in such reverence.

Thus, he often said, hoisting his beer aloft: "To Western Medicine!"

EM

The Work. Another enigmatic phrase that we struggled to limn. The Work. What an overburdened word. Work, with all its puritanical self-righteousness, all its negative connotations of burden. What you're supposed to do, for some reason, though nobody bothers to explain why. As if it's self-evident. But he often reversed directions to reveal new meanings hidden behind the old. Work was indeed work, but more encompassing. It was everything you chose to do. So flipping burgers at the diner was work. But attention made all the difference. It could be mere employment, but it could also be the necessary support to The Work. What really needed to be done, what was really necessary, became not work, that generic noun, but The Work, always with the definitive article, always that delineation, to distinguish it from that other necessity of existence in a society that demanded money. Because The Work was not an antidote to work. The Work liberated, while the other, the one without the article's specificity, confined. But insights gleaned from even the most repetitive and banal task, even especially from the most repetitive and banal task, had a place in The Work as well. Everything fed The Work, even if every moment might not be worthy. Everything contributed. But ultimately, there was something, something important, that needed to be done—an expanding, multiplying, engaging—and that, in the end, was The Work.

CK

An alchemical marriage of opposites, the synthesis of man and woman to become a third thing—in his words "a hermaphrodite"—that's what Ryan advised. To those who listened, he said, "Become as a child." This notion was always vague. I understood "be open and curious," but the ambiguousness of his words made me think there was more to it. For a long time, Ryan's "child" idea plagued me. It was like a code I needed to break, or a riddle with multiple meanings. I ruminated on it for a long time. Then, several years later, I heard a Christmas carol playing in a restaurant in Portland, Oregon. Snow fell outside as I realized his genius.

"Said the night wind to the little lamb,
do you see what I see?"

The lyrics jumped out at me and I understood.

"Said the little lamb to the shepherd boy,
do you hear what I hear?"

At that moment, "Do You Hear What I Hear?" became profound. For the first time, I realized the words referenced more than Jesus. In fact, maybe the song wasn't about Him at all. Like most religious expressions, this had many layers.

"Said the shepherd boy to the mighty king,
do you know what I know?"

Long after the restaurant, the lyrics reverberated with me. Haunting, until I dug deeper. I became a detective of sorts, trying to unravel his puzzle. After a lot of digging, I discovered that when the poets mentioned Childe Roland or Childe Harold, they were referring to Arthurian legend, referring to knights as Sir. Ryan was telling us to become like knights, to find our towers, to find our grails. This research led to many discoveries. It opened a world with many occult tributaries, spokes that all led back to Mystical Christianity. I saw his lineage. I discovered the allegory of the Bible. The Gnostics, the Rosicrucians, the Freemasons, Crowley's Thelemites, all these are forms of Mystical Christianity and alchemical magic, with its main branch leading back to Ancient Egypt (Al-Kheme meaning "black land" in Arabic). Alchemy led to an immortality of spirit.

His eternalness was that he drew upon these traditions. That's what made him out of time. When people live deep in the capitalist mindset, fashion, speech, and attitudes become dated to the time in which the individuals were indoctrinated. They can't break out of this conditioning because purchases and media programming define their style:

Hipsters, Goths, Punks, Hippies, Yuppies, or Millennials. Not him. Timelessness defined his approach. His language, his philosophical research, his spirituality, all stemmed from a black river, something deep within the soul, where the stars shine bright, where every person is a star.

His mission came into perspective. In my mind, he became a knight-errant on an absurd holy mission like Don Quixote. His giants were the windmills of the global capitalist mindset, the selfish trappings of that worldview. His power channeled 5,000-year-old magic. He was a child because he lived absolutely in the present, yet he carried the knowledge of the ages.

EM

What Ryan really offered was a new relationship with the self. Not just self-understanding, which though difficult, could be achieved in a number of ways. Not self-control, or the ability to force one part of the self to do the bidding of the other. Not a false sense of self-aggrandizement built on an inflated notion of one's capabilities either. More than these, Ryan provided a sense of one's own power derived from a true faith in the innermost worth, dignity, and possibility of the individual. Though people claim to either possess or offer this very same thing all the time, it's really very difficult to achieve.

And it was exactly what I needed to discover. In yoga there is much talk about the "center," and "balance" is a catchword throughout our culture. But what Ryan taught was not just a matter of finding an inner peace or equilibrium (though that was part of it), or silencing the cacophony of the outside world. It was something even more ambitious.

It was about bringing out the power that was already within so that it could work an effect on the world. I had been searching outside myself, looking for the idea that would bring meaning into my life. Ryan helped me to discover the meaning that was already within, waiting to be released. One just needed the courage and guidance to honestly confront the true nature of the self.

It was largely a function of attention. A simple question of self-reflection: to what do you give your attention? To your job, your spouse, your kids, your television? None of these were wrong—in fact in his cosmos the word "wrong" was oddly absent—it was instead a matter of recognizing what exactly you were doing, thinking, feeling at any given moment. That was the starting place. Truly acknowledging what it was that was going on inside you. It amazed me not only how difficult that actually was, but how that act of realization immediately opened a new door that you could step out of if you desired. Or not. Do I really want to keep playing this video game, keep drinking this beer, keep fretting about this worry? Once you recognized what you were doing in each moment, accepted it, and went on to truly attend to this experience, it was strange how often you found yourself deciding to change the pattern, to redirect. To put your attention somewhere else.

At times Ryan spoke in a psychological manner, turning your questions back on you like a therapist, asking you to determine why you might have asked that or what that query reveals about yourself. He could, when appropriate, invoke theory. He was well read in the scholarship without being pedantic. But such invocations were only there to stimulate thought, to provide another angle—he never relied on the weight of the past, or even less, on authority. But the framing of discussions, the way in which questions and statements were propounded, caught his ear. Thus everything said or thought or proposed became the starting point for self-critique, the key to unlocking a door inside yourself that you never knew existed.

His most important talent was an ability to listen. He was always attentive, waiting patiently for the right bit of information to emerge. I can't stress how important this was, this waiting. So many people pretend to listen while only waiting for an opportunity to interject their ego into the conversation. He listened like a psychologist might listen, but his science was farther afield. The psychologist looks for neurosis in order to heal it. Ryan didn't want to heal your craziness. For him it represented an opening: he wanted to encourage it, to cultivate this eccentricity, to transform it into something new.

Ryan's intensity meant that you always had to struggle to repossess yourself. Not that he absconded with it. By no means. When you were with him you gave it freely, like breathing in deeply for the doctor. But with him it was your soul under consideration. Your essence. What made you you, why you did the things you did. Your being. He had a knack for understanding it. For picking it up, examining its several sides, noticing inconsistencies, then giving it back. Unlike a doctor, however, he would never diagnose. Only prescribe. You had to name your own disease.

Yet that didn't lessen the anxiety (at times mind you, at times) that perhaps his influence was too great. Oh, but he only listens. Oh, but he's helped me find myself. True and still, at those odd intervals, the mind wondered. Has he pulled me from my orbit? But then what was I orbiting before?

Ryan's method of teaching was not for everyone. The brutal nature of his method turned off many. Not everyone wanted to unveil their soul to him for inspection, much less to themselves for change. It could be a treacherous road. Ryan always advised against succumbing to fear but fear is difficult to overcome, and terrifying to confront. But the entire point of the process was to face fear, to face the dark shadows of your own mind, body, and soul, in order to learn from and accept the full reality of the self. Detroit, in many ways, was simply the physical correlative of the uncertainties we faced in ourselves. It was easy enough to talk about empowerment and trusting oneself, but shining a light into the dark recesses of the soul often proved too much. Others simply found the entire method too difficult to undertake. I myself struggled (and continue to struggle) with maintaining this attitude toward life, and even today wonder if I am still on the path.

But what troubled him, and his philosophy, is that many people still chose to say yes to a second-hand world, even after their attention recognized its objects. He had a hard time with this fact. How could you have a revolution—and he really did want a revolution—when many were content with the gildings and trappings of their own mental cage? Were they simply too deeply programmed for a moment of clarity to alter their desires, or was another technique for bringing them to attention undiscovered or, even worse, lacking? Were some simply incapable of the true freedom he was offering?

EM

If there was ever a weakness in his magical teachings it was the curious temptation numbers held for him. The primary understanding of magic as attention was his ineluctable mantra and with that I felt a full concordance. That life was what I decided to focus on seemed an irrefutable truth. But numbers attached to this precept oddly. That threes and fours repeated because I looked for threes and fours was above reproach. But that three meant instability while four meant balance went beyond me (well, not beyond me, through me, let's say, or perhaps by me. Yes, by me, without touching). Why did numbers afflict him so? To answer that question took you down a dark path. Toward conundrum and paradox, a cul-de-sac where thoughts, bandied about as if in an eddy, circulated endlessly.

CK

I suspect Ryan's fascination with numbers stemmed from his interest in the Qabalah and the technique of reading the numerical value of letters called Gematria. In the science, every letter has a value attributed to it. One can read the numbers as if they're a language and derive meaning from numerical correspondences. Hence, Crowley's obsession with numbers like 777 and 666 stems from Greek phrases translated as "I am the resurrection (777)" and "Mark of the Beast (666)."

These numbers represent deep significance to spiritual scholars. Like in the film *Pi*, some posit that God is communicating, revealing that the Bible acts as a numerical cipher that holds untold magical secrets and the stories convey an exoteric shell hiding an esoteric meaning.

In the beginning was the Word... but the beginning starts with a letter, strung into words. With this idea, Ryan's fascination with sigils becomes meaningful. If numbers and letters can have magical power, a magician can change reality.

This isn't a crazy idea if you imagine letters as energy. Reality is a large computer. Computers take commands as numerical code and the code produces words, images, and sounds. By inputting a command, you change the machine's output. The computer (the universe) doesn't change. The inherent laws built into the system stay the same but the words, images, and sounds change the magician and his or her circumstances. Think of the universe as one large brain and then you can see how we might be synapses contributing to the functioning or direction of the larger organism.

When people call someone a man of letters, this takes on a deeper meaning. Words like *abracadabra* have power because of their numerical significance. In creating a sigil, a magician states a desire by writing it down, by spelling it, by crafting a "spell." Scribes it into reality. Remove the vowels to simplify the letter string, to make them more potent. Arrange the letters into a symbol. The alphanumeric cipher, letters bound up with numbers, projects into reality as a command. The command changes reality. Considering Pi, the Golden Ratio, as a numerical command with perfect balance, a spiral harmony in all of nature, one can see how God creates.

In this light, Ryan's passion for numbers was a passion for reality, a way of digging deeper into the possibilities of awareness. He understood our reality as an unfathomable machine, a psycho-energized omni-computer. In my mind's eye, I can see him meditating. I can imagine the minutiae of numbers and letters spiraling through his consciousness creating a fingerprint of the cosmos, a double of the Milky Way, and then drifting off. I can imagine him losing himself to the divine as the alphanumeric code flows into the collective unconscious. His eyes open and I witness absolute trust in a system most people doubt.

Absolute trust in the universe as a playmate.

EM

Some might say it's hardest to be true to others but really, it's hardest to be true to yourself. To not lie. It would seem like bullshitting others would be easiest but actually bullshitting yourself takes place daily, maybe hourly. Maybe all the time. Ryan never bullshit anyone, especially himself. Sometimes I wonder if that was what was behind it all in the end. Pure unadulterated truth at all times. No bullshit. A sacred trust never to be broken. This truth looked a lot like fearlessness. And it was. The ability to be honest with yourself is rare and requires one to look deep inside with the light on and eyes wide open. You could tell by his bearing, his words, and his face that Ryan had looked.

Ryan preached a policy of honesty. Which is not always an honest policy. His own honesty was both shield and weapon. When turned on himself, it ensured a purity of purpose that was essential in his quest. How could he achieve anything lying to himself? Yet it could also be brutal when turned outward, especially when someone had little experience with bald fact and unmitigated opinion. It irritated many, vexed a lot, and cowed quite a few. But why would a man who, it is true, made a living as a salesman, resort to such candor? Duplicity takes a psychic toll on its user; how easier it is to always tell the truth. And how powerful. And, yes, sometimes, how mean.

CK

He understood honesty as the key to most of the world's troubles. All our miseries arise from our struggles with honesty. These problems contribute to the ego's self-deception.

Ryan saw all lies similarly; petty lies, like lying to a lover about their fashion, equated with great lies like the ideologies of governments. He accepted these as unavoidable evils in order for society to continue. Sometimes, lies are necessary, but lying to oneself is always unforgivable. Authenticity is most important, especially within our hearts. People hated him for this reason. His honesty reflected their deceit. It revealed deficiency and flaws. It revealed what one needed to work toward. Of course, he had his own weaknesses. He certainly did. But he rolled with those. Weaknesses didn't concern him much because they were part of his package. Ryan reveled in contradiction, so naturally, he saw his own flaws as strengths. He threw them out there. Many times, he told women he wanted to sleep with them. No finesse about it. No beating around the bush. He told them like it was an obvious fact. People couldn't handle it. He told you if something was terrible. That painting you did? It sucked. But when he praised something, it was genuine.

CK

Ryan brought over a battered videotape of Kenneth Anger's films *Invocation of My Demon Brother* and *Lucifer Rising*. Each film contained symbolism inspired by the Golden Dawn. I should have slept, but his excitement inspired my irresponsibility. I humored him though I'd regret it the next morning. He popped it into the VCR and hit play. The static tuned to wavy lines, and the video started. He turned and smirked. Egyptian iconography, occult symbolism, and psychedelia merged on screen and they drew me into the abstract narrative. Images of ceremonial rites and desert madness struck me. The magic scenes became obvious on some level, but I failed to understand the symbolism. I did, however, see the connection to Jungian psychology and alchemy. At that point, I had read a few of Jung's books and studied archetypes in my mythology class at Macomb Community College.

Did Ryan perform magic on me? Did he program me with the video? Was there more to this? Perhaps he knew the images would stick in my mind. I'll never know for certain, but I accepted his stance on magic more seriously after that night. The video churned something deep inside. Images can mutate thought, and I was devouring them. Alex's torture in *A Clockwork Orange* and the snuff film's effect on people in *Videodrome* come to mind. Was Ryan planting suggestions in my brain? Re-educating me? It's possible. It's difficult to say. On one level, he brought over a cool thing to watch. But with hindsight, I wonder. He exposed me to so many things that became important aspects in my life. Sometimes he taught me but I didn't understand until later. An example of this: Genesis P-Orridge meeting William S. Burroughs. Burroughs chatted with Genesis in front of the Beat writer's television and while they spoke Burroughs flipped through the channels in succession making cut-ups of the broadcasts. P-Orridge realized Burroughs revealed magic through the telecasts' juxtapositions. Ryan was a huge fan of both men so it's possible he was doing something similar.

Ryan's interest in symbolism was like his interest in numbers and letters. Symbols were alive to him. Potent ideas conveying deep thought. What was the symbolism of volcanoes erupting, crocodiles hatching from eggs, and magi performing arcane rituals doing to my brain? It's difficult to say, but I'm certain he showed the video to trigger latent ideas. It wasn't about art. It was about transformation.

And that's where this becomes more interesting because if I ignored those hints, those symbolic video breadcrumbs, I might not be the person I am today. It shows the importance of each action. How many times does a friend bring over a movie? How many times does it have intent beyond entertainment? That separated Ryan from others. Everything was about intent, and once you realized, you wondered about his motives. What did he want you to see?

EM

He had doubts about the efficacy of his teachings. But never any doubts about the teachings themselves. Never. The test of the surety of his method is that while I often doubt whether I have stayed on the path, I have never doubted the truth of his teachings. They remain a standard by which I can measure my thoughts and actions. But the man, like all of us, had his failings. Though he taught the path, he was also on it himself, and would often wander off into the forest, questioning what the true way was, the decisions he made, and his ability to remain true to himself. Thus, he was more like a fellow traveler than a guru, one always slightly farther ahead, but subject to disappear as the path twisted, turned, and became overgrown.

You would find yourself wondering, sometimes, what would he do? What would he do in this situation? Then wonder if the wondering what he would do is precisely what he wouldn't do, and wouldn't want you to do either.

"Do what you do," heard from a Black man late one night in a Detroit gas station, was something he advised often and repeatedly.

I always admired his commitment to the suburbs. Many loved them for the wrong reasons. And many tried to escape to the city. But he stayed. He knew his place. He was not always sure of those he taught, or their worthiness. He questioned their capacities for truly understanding his words. But he continued, firm in the conviction of his path, even if he inevitably outpaced his pupils, stopping always to help, to lend a shoulder, but ultimately always too fast for them to stay apace. They littered the roadside of his pedagogy.

Was he lonely? The time spent aimlessly driving, meditating at home, secluded in his room, did it ever weigh on him? There was forbearance about him. Not complacency, nothing could be farther than that, but a stilled acceptance that was at most times Buddhist but could slip into a hint of catatonia, a spaced-out quality to his eyes, in his less attentive moments. A resting? Let's call it a pausing.

EM

The uncomfortable truth is that I temporarily left Detroit for a relationship. Despite my desire to distance myself from romantic entanglements in order to see who I really was (and who I really could be), after some time alone I became involved with someone else. Tina was amazing, and the more I got to know this woman, the more interested I became. She was a graduate student in Psychology, and we would spend long days working together at a café, and then go out for long nights at the bar with friends. Tina was smart, ambitious, and we could spend hours bringing our different fields into dialogue and even sometimes into synthesis. I admired her work ethic, and she was clearly destined for great things in her profession. Tina lived in the posh suburb of Royal Oak, and it was a nice break from the struggle that was Detroit. But a pleasant year was undercut by the knowledge that she would be accepting a post-doctoral position at the University of Washington that summer. As she took off for Seattle, I was left with the choice of remaining in Detroit to struggle alone, or following her in the hopes of getting a job and making things work. So, I packed up and moved into a small Seattle apartment with her. I figured that with the growth I already experienced, I would not lose myself in my partner like I had done so many times before. We were really in love.

Things started out fine. After Detroit it was amazing to live in a functioning city. The bus stops actually had a time-table posted, and even more surprising, the buses actually arrived on time. It was in many ways an idyllic existence. I had fellowship money, so I focused on finishing my dissertation, exploring the city, and loving Tina.

But there were struggles as well, ones very different than in Detroit. Seattle made things almost too easy. I missed the challenges of Detroit, the pitting oneself against the raw elements. The cozy, liberal, educated vibe of Seattle made it an ideal place to reside. You were surrounded by your same element. Detroit offered resistance, but it was precisely in the act of struggling that you could find yourself. Seattle simply confirmed what you already thought you were.

In many ways it wasn't Seattle's fault. Joining a partner already established meant that I was already once-removed from everything I encountered. I found friends, but mainly through Tina's network. I existed between tourist and resident, like someone spending a year abroad in a foreign country. More than just passing through, but not really establishing permanent roots. Life sort of glided by, unsatisfactorily.

As fall started to arrive, I found myself without a job and without prospects. Our relationship suffered because of this malaise, and I became anxious. I turned my sight back east again, thinking on Detroit. Returning began to make more and more sense. There was unfinished business, and since Detroit was where it started, it seemed the appropriate place to finish. Tina was of course dismayed, but admitted to me one night, "If I was you I probably wouldn't have come out here." We were two academics struggling to balance our love for each other with our personal and professional ambitions.

I returned to Detroit. Fortunately, I was able to find work teaching classes at local universities part time. For the first week I actually stayed with Ryan in his suburban apartment complex. He was reticent and it was a strange experience. By this time he had found a job, so I had afternoons to read Jorge Luis Borges by the pool while I waited for him to get off work. Our conversations picked up where they had left off, as always, but I could tell my presence was difficult for him. He needed his private space, his sanctuary. What started as a pleasant stay, a sort of prolonged "sleep over," had become strained and I pushed harder to find a place of my own, so as not to taint our relationship.

Detroit was no longer an option. It was the crucible that had helped shape me, but it was almost too much. The struggle for survival, to find an onion that wasn't rotten, to sit in a café and sip a hot coffee, to not be accosted with pleas for money or rides or psychic energy, had gotten to be too much. I needed somewhere that offered that edge experience that could push me, but without exhausting me to the point of collapse like Detroit had often done.

Ryan put me back into contact with Chris, and we decided to room together. It would turn out to be a perfect match. He too had spent productive time in Detroit and was likewise both energized and wearied by the struggle. We spent a number of days trying to think of the best area in Detroit for the sort of growth we desired. After much discussion, soul searching, and bonding, we decided on Hamtramck.

We moved into the upper flat of a dilapidated home where the first thing I noticed were the walls. The apartment was on the second floor of an old 1920s tenement home, originally a house for several generations of family but subsequently divided in two and rented out by our slumlord Mike. It looked like they had made it the rumpus room for the kids, as if they had moved the cheap fake-wood paneling and horrible shag carpeting in your average Midwestern basement up to the second floor. Cracked linoleum covered the kitchen and bathroom. It had a stove from the 1960s and an even older refrigerator. Two bedrooms were located off to the side, and there was what was once a parlor or sitting room with a bay window in the front. After living three years in a basement, I immediately took that. Chris holed himself up in a dark back room, warm and protected.

The windows made the place acceptable. We froze in the winter and burned in the summer, but at least we had light and a view, if you can call it that. We looked out on other neighbors, and across from us was a vacant lot that I pretended was a slice of nature. Through the lot you could see the backs of the houses in the next block over, all boarded up and slumping. Only one had any activity, a ramshackle place that we later learned was a crackhouse. It felt like we were sailing above the block on a precarious cutter, listing to the side trying to stay upright.

Our crow's nest was the balcony, a dilapidating platform cut into the corner of the house. The guardrail was too low and about to fall off, but there was an all-weather couch from which you could survey the neighborhood. All the action took place in the street. Two doors down you could watch the effeminate Polish teenager clandestinely look around before jumping into his sugar daddy's car. Bangladeshi kids huddled around a rat flattened to comic book proportions. A scraggly pack of wild dogs trotted by from the abandoned woodlots and fields that were interspersed among the junkyards and warehouses to our north. And our downstairs neighbors conducted their always-too-public rants. Or you could just sit and let the sun bake your face.

An old Polish enclave, Hamtramck was Detroit's antithesis. Surrounded by Detroit itself, it was a relative oasis, like the ones we had been forming but on a larger scale. Detroit was uni-cultural, but Hamtramck contained everybody—Poles, Serbians, Croatians, Bangladeshi, Arab-Americans and Blacks as well. The high school had students speaking over forty languages. But it would be wrong to call it a model of multiculturalism.

The fact is that Hamtramck worked because it followed an older model of racial segregation. Every group had its own quarter, with the main drag, Joseph Campau street, a sort of common zone. Not that you couldn't enter another group's area. You could. But there was a palpable sense of propriety, and you knew you were somewhere that wasn't technically yours. It felt like what I imagine a younger America must have felt like—a world of everybody keeping to their own. The irony of this separate-but-relatively-equal development was that it worked. As long as you knew the rules and played by them everybody got along.

We lived at the edge of the Bangladeshi and Arab quarters, and our liminal position between these two groups made our block something like an experiment. Our downstairs neighbors were white and seemed to exist on the periphery of respectability. A sister took care of her disabled brother who had been shot. At any hour of the day or night his friends would arrive, loud and racist and usually with something stolen in the back of their truck. Next door was a Bangladeshi family, with an old man who grew mint among spilt crankcase oil in the backyard. I once offered my hand after talking to him and he extended his fist for me to grab. On the other side were Poles, and across the street was a Black family three generations strong. The grandmother would sit on the porch in the heat of summer with a parka, sunning herself. Farther down, in a house painted bright maroon, was an Arab family who would yell at the Polish kids who used the abandoned lot as a baseball field. From our second story balcony there was always something to see—"street theatre" at its finest.

Hamtramck offered much the same environment as Detroit, but because it was more densely populated, it afforded important amenities that the city lacked. There was a grocery store, and a nice café for doing work. The bus routes weren't great, and you had to transfer in order to get downtown. But it was precisely the sort of sanctuary we were seeking, and cheap. We decided to base ourselves there and make daily forays into the city.

Our time in Hamtramck was a period of gathering strength, of testing our powers, of consolidating our position. Ryan was instrumental in this change, but by the end of our time here, his presence was diminishing. The truth is, he started coming around less and less. Part of this was the direction we took. Chris and I had become extroverted in ways that Ryan disapproved of. He saw this sociality as a distraction, and in a way it was. Exhausted by Detroit, we decided to move in a new direction, displaying rather than cultivating the lessons he had sown.

I could certainly see Ryan's point. Maybe we had taken on too much too soon, like a kid at Christmas who wants to run outside and ride a new bike in the snow. I've seen the same behavior in some of my own students. We had absorbed Ryan's lessons, but were they integrated deep enough to sustain lasting change? Would we be lured back to distraction by the effects of the power he had helped us to uncover? Ryan cautioned us, and while we understood his fears, we also felt that the time had come to move on, regardless of the danger.

CK

Invisible Polish and Serbian mafia boundaries kept Detroit hooligans at bay, so a calmness existed on the streets. Our move became a respite from the chaos of the Cass Corridor—a blossoming.

Leaving soul-searching behind me, I took on an extroverted lifestyle. I gained confidence in work, play, and love. I became a member of the bohemian underbelly that comprised artists, writers, musicians, academics, and outcasts. A different phase began. A time where I became a teacher to others. Ryan and I faced difficulties because this new outlook created a wedge between student and teacher. Perhaps it was the student rebelling against the teacher. Or perhaps, the student diverged down a different path. Regardless, there was still more to learn.

Many of the conversations Ryan and I had over the past year echoed through my mind as I put the wisdom gleaned from these exchanges into practice. My new perspective involved research into the occult, a more assertive will, and a reexamining of where I needed to go as an awakened individual. I was alert and ready for new avenues of exploration.

Understanding magic and its manifestations gave me a stronger will to move through life with a purpose. I didn't sign on to Thelema like Ryan but it inspired me. People responded to my stronger energy as I became more integrated in the local art and literary scene. I focused more on writing and producing handmade books. I took classes at the Center for Creative Studies to learn printing and bookbinding. I took part in art exhibits. I adopted a stronger creative identity. A wakefulness I never experienced made my interactions with people more substantial. And magic played a large role in this.

As I ventured into society, away from the solitude I experienced the previous year, every meeting had an undercurrent of synchronicity and a secret clash of wills became commonplace. I attuned my awareness to these subtleties, and I used them. I made friendships that mirrored my relationship with Ryan, but I became a guide, rather than a student.

CK

The Great Work is difficult to realize in this ego-driven world. Working with the psychological problems that people threw upon Ryan's shoulders became a great burden, and I never envied his position. This spiritual midwifery he wove carried a high cost, and it manifested with mood swings.

Like so many of his contradictions, aggression and serenity clashed within him. For the most part, he was patient. Yet sometimes, I saw him explode with fury. He could lose it when a person didn't understand what he was trying to express, especially when it concerned abstract occult ideas that took him years to grasp. Trying to distill this into a single conversation was a daunting task.

One such experience happened years prior at The Movies at Lakeside. The late-night shift found Ryan as the box office cashier and myself a closing usher. The final movies ran, and he closed up the register. His high school girlfriend, Kara, came in for a visit. They chatted in front of the box office and their voices grew louder. Ryan exited the cubicle and walked away from her to take the money to the main office. I chatted with Kara while he counted the cash inside the room. She was a difficult person to read so I couldn't figure out what happened. He came out and they walked back to the box office, so he could gather his stuff. Their conversation became heated.

With a shrug, I heard her say, "That's just the way it is. You have to live with it."

In a flurry of anger, he smashed his fist through the box office glass, and ran down the hall into the closed shopping mall. A blood trail followed him. With her fists clenched, she stormed out the mall entrance. Several ushers chased after him. We tracked his blood trail down the hall until we found him clutching his hand. He wasn't crying. Not a tear of pain, just this intense glare directed into space. As we gathered him up, he said, "She slept with him, my best friend."

He was never the same because she destroyed a part of him that night. Did the spiritual insights he gave his tribe backfire? Maybe his experiments into polygamy came back to haunt him. Before this event, his eyes carried warmth. After, he adopted a cold, steely glint.

EM

Hamtramck's social scene was fueled by alcohol and music. We lived around the corner from Small's, a club that hosted a wide range of Detroit music but focused mainly on a rockabilly sound that seeped out of Detroit's working-class Southern roots. But the majority of Hamtramck's bars offered their own take on the Detroit music scene, from electronica to reggae, depending on the venue and night. Anything could happen. I was on a date one night when I suggested to my partner that we stop at the Polish Village Café for a nightcap. This venerable basement eatery offered solid Polish fare in the day, but at night I would often go there to hear a jazz trio of old Polish men play smooth standards while I sipped my Zywiec in the corner. So when

I saw the dim light coming from the basement I thought we might catch their house band. It was these sorts of serendipitous moments that made me love Detroit. When I was exploring San Francisco or New York there were almost too many choices. It felt like everything was going on all the time, right around the corner. But Detroit had the element of surprise, making chance encounters with people or places all the more special because they were unexpected. When we had descended the stairs, I saw that the place was empty, save for a cluster of people around the end of the bar. So I went up and ordered. The bartender told me that it was a private party we had stumbled into, and that she'd have to ask Jack if it was all right for us to have a drink. As she walked over to the cluster, I realized why the place seemed so odd. Everyone was huddled around one guy with his back to the bar. I mean really close to him, and nobody was engaged in side conversations. It reminded me of Ryan—he commanded full attention. The bartender returned, said it was fine, and asked what I wanted. I ordered two beers, and when I tried to pay, I was told that it was on the house. I sauntered back to my excited date, who leaned over close to me as I sat down, and said, "I think that's Jack White at the bar!"

CK

Vice, parties, and fellowship filled our time in Hamtramck. Whether it was drinking alcohol, experimenting with psychedelics, or playing around sexually, we pushed the envelope.

One experience involved three hits of acid scored from a guy in the kitchen at the Cass Café. Excited, I mentioned it to Betty, a free-spirit friend-with-benefits, who sat at the bar waiting for me to finish my shift. Like many women in Detroit, she was tough as nails with her thrift store chic and sharp intellect.

I said, "We should do it tonight."

She fiddled with her rucksack and asked, "Where should we drop it?"

I answered, "We could head to my place. It's safe enough there with a good vibe."

A few minutes later, we hopped into a Checker cab and headed to my house.

We burst into the flat with laughter. Erik was reading in his room. After some salutations, I whipped out the acid paper with a quizzical look. My eyes said, "You interested?" After a second of hesitation, he agreed. Without delay, we dropped the LSD.

We grabbed a few beers from the fridge and plopped down on our old couch in the living room. I put on a Buffy Sainte-Marie record. We chatted for a few minutes. Made small talk. The drug took hold.

I looked at Betty and watched her pupils dilate. She was a beautiful woman with a dark side that manifested in a quirky sense of humor. The drug made me see this more. I wanted to have sex with her at that moment, but the situation prevented it. The drug muddled our brains, and sex would have been impossible in that state.

We went over the edge as the acid yanked us about. We tripped hard as the conversation flowed, meandering around different topics and emotions. One second, we focused with clarity, concentrating on analyzing the room's minutiae. The next second, we became babbling fools wondering when the trip would end.

During the journey we talked about many things both mundane and lofty. All of us were avid readers and into the arts, so discussion developed. This was common ground for Erik and me, but Betty's fresh perspective complemented our ongoing discussion.

We discussed *Bulfinch's Mythology*, a book that became my obsession. Our discussion ambled along through the great powers of the ancient world. We talked of the gods and goddesses not as personalities, but as potencies that influenced people and breathed holiness into reality. Back then, societies believed in these powers as affecting existence directly, not in a dull, allegorical manner the way they're viewed today.

The record player churned out tunes as we talked of anthropology and the tarot. Mystic arts and *The Cloud of Unknowing*. The manic jazz of Charles Mingus and Eric Dolphy. Bliss and the Devil. Psychedelic journeys into oblivion.

Then, our discussion moved on to Erik's Soviet military hat from his bedroom. We chatted about his time living in Russia. He was gifted the hat along with an overcoat that represented a connection to the place, and the object's Soviet-ness was interesting because it relayed a different time and attitude, one far removed from American capitalism. On and on we journeyed though our trip, and the conversation itself became a tangled web: gooey and difficult to escape.

Hours passed.

We peaked as the conversation turned to intimate thoughts. Lovers long gone. Our hopes and fears. Death.

The sun came up. More than once, I tried to maneuver Betty into my bedroom to have sex. This never happened, but she and I went to my room to discuss wigs. Sometimes she played a game where she went to a random bar disguised in some ridiculous outfit as a goofy character. People believed the disguise but knew something was off. I accompanied her once, and it was a blast. Riding the wave of acid, we giggled about the subterfuge.

Erik remained in his room thinking about God knows what and probably wondering what we were laughing at.

After a time, we realized our unit worked best as a trio. Still laughing, we called to Erik. The three of us reunited near the balcony. The dawn's light came through the front door's window like shards penetrating another dimension. Betty's eyes welled up with tears of joy. Erik gazed out at the sunrise's majesty. I stared at the veins pulsing on my hand. We felt at peace, but ready for movement. More than once, we tried to leave the house. Something stopped us—either fear or we had more to say. As we continued the conversation, the sun wrapped around us, warming our thoughts and inspiring us even more to venture out into the exhilarating morning.

After more tries, we finally moved, and it liberated us.

Outside, the idea came to find food. We walked to Campau looking for an open restaurant. Not sure if we ever found nourishment or if we could even eat in our heightened state, but leaving our second story sanctuary became a potent symbol for me. It represented an exit from Detroit. All of us were trying to break free of the city's gravity and soon life would propel us in different directions.

EM

We were living in Hamtramck, but Detroit was still very much a center for us. Hamtramck had its café where I would write, and some bars, but it was far more of a reprieve from the vicissitudes of the city than the crucible that Detroit represented. I remember one evening in particular when Ryan and I went down to see some electronica music at The Gold Dollar. The club was really nothing more than a long bar with part of a corner given over to a stage. I had been a few times before, with the bands being a pretext to see a bartender who would flirt with me without ever actually going out. But Ryan suggested music, and it sounded like a good idea. If she was there, that would only be a bonus.

We arrived and ordered two beers. Detroit electronica is not about the stage performance typically. Two guys were behind a table adjusting various dials and moving levers up and down. The effects of these machinations were not immediately apparent to me. The music was acceptable, but there seemed a curiously frantic element to the performance. The various synthesizers seemed always on the verge of doing something "wrong," and the musicians appeared more like technicians struggling to impede some sort of meltdown. The Gold Dollar was notoriously loud, and claimed a sort of status as a bar where one went to hear music, not to chat while music was being played. But I could tell without speaking that Ryan was picking up on what I was feeling as well. After some time watching the show, he smiled wryly, leaned toward me, and said, "It looks like they are placating the machine!"

EM

A defining moment—Ryan's girlfriend Mandy on my bed. She was a beautifully seductive redheaded woman, very petite but overflowing with vitality. With all the time spent together, Mandy and I had become close friends, and we would often go off together to talk. She was a sculptor, a potter, an artist who liked making interesting assemblages from everyday material. As with all of us, Ryan was her catalyst. But she also chronicled how frustrating it was to be in a sexual relationship with such a man, and I saw another side of my friend, one fraught with indecision and confusion as Ryan strove to reconcile his belief in open relationships with issues of envy and jealousy. So when she stretched across my bed luxuriously while arching her back so slightly and rolling gently to her side in nothing but her light cotton panties, I was sorely tempted. And out of a duty in my head I said no.

Ryan had a habit of trading partners. It was never crassly discussed. On the contrary, he always made it sound like the most enlightened and obvious decision possible. He said he would have been all right with it, and in fact, it had already been discussed between them. But it also felt a bit calculated. The fact was that though Mandy had wanted to be with me, Ryan's desire to experiment with another woman he had brought to our place was the real catalyst for the occasion. While it sounds callous, it is likewise true that Ryan himself was often at odds with himself and his own actions, as he discussed with me on numerous occasions. Mandy and Ryan had been in a dialogue for months over whether she should become an exotic dancer, and while Ryan felt it would be good for her to "explore" that side of desire and it would certainly mean much money, he also knew that his motives were not beyond suspicion, since her job would help pay for his expenses. They were torn, and the fact that she eventually took a position at a strip club did nothing to alleviate the difficulties, but compounded them.

So, while he said that it would have been fine for me to sleep with Mandy, I know that on another level, it wouldn't have been. Despite an avowed liberalism born of both theory and practice, he was more than capable of jealousy.

And I don't blame him. But I do think he always trusted me after that.

CK

Chatting in the living room was common because of the record player, but our place was a party house since we had a balcony and three bedrooms. Privacy was possible with many nooks and crannies to explore. Erik's bedroom was at the front of the house near the balcony. My room sat at the rear next to the kitchen. In the middle, an extra bedroom acted as a library. Bookcases, boxes, junk overflow, and a futon complemented art that we didn't showcase in the living room.

Tunes played as we chatted about Albert Camus, William Blake, or some other writer. After twenty minutes of chit-chat, the conversation turned to other topics. On impulse, Ryan got up and bolted into the library. We followed him. He scanned the book titles as the rest of us talked. I watched him as he took an interest in two masks on the wall. One was a Balinese Barong demon, and the other was a Day of the Dead Calaca skull with Meh-hee-koh stamped on the back. My ex-wife Gayle bought the masks at Pier One Imports, a store where people bought things from countries where they have never been. Somehow, I ended up with the crap after the divorce. Anyhow, Ryan took a shine to the demon mask, comparing the fiery black-and-red lioness visage to the cover of the traditional Balinese music LP playing in the living room. My anarchist taxi driver, the guy who drove me home from work most nights, gifted me the record while we chatted about Bernardine Dohrn and The Weather Underground.

As the drinks flowed, the whole room became a little salacious. Mandy acted this way most of the time and the alcohol only increased her candor. Eventually, Ryan pushed us from the room stating, "Time for The Work."

Erik and I returned to the living room, a little annoyed with his behavior. Silence ensued behind the closed library door. After a few moments, moans came from the room. At first low feminine moans, but then after a few moments we heard him too. We pretended not to listen, but that was impossible, so we smirked at each other. As they got more into having sex, his moans became muffled. This became a curiosity. What was going on in there? She panted louder as he performed The Work. A few minutes later, the door swung open, and they emerged, flush and out of breath. They strolled into the living room like nothing happened. We all laughed to ease the awkward moment. Our little gathering resumed.

A few days later, Ryan and I chatted in The Clock Restaurant. That night came up.

Without modesty, Ryan explained, "I invoked a Balinese demon to fuck Mandy. I wore that fucking demon mask the whole time like an avatar."

I studied him as he spoke, wondering where this was going. He fidgeted with his coffee mug.

He looked out the window into the parking lot and added, "I took her from behind and she loved it."

I asked, "Did you do it to get your kicks or was there a magical purpose?"

He grinned and said, "Magicians never know the outcome. Do the ritual. Then, just wait and see."

I nodded. I watched a homeless guy fiddle with a newspaper box.

I said, "I understand that, but was there a purpose?"

He answered, "The ritual was a magical working I developed, something to do with Babalon, or at least an extension."

I didn't quite understand what he meant. He tried to explain. He talked of Gematria, numerical correspondence, and Crowley. At first, I thought he was referring to the city Babylon.

"No, that's not it," he said and added, "turns out I'm trying to invoke Armageddon by using Mandy, my Scarlet Woman, but also esoterically named Babalon."

This conversation meant nothing to me. Years later, while reading about Jack Parsons, the occultist who helped invent the rocket fuel that got us to the moon, I came across the 1946 Babalon Working, where Parsons performed sex magic rituals by having intercourse with his Scarlet Woman: the artist, poet, actress, and occultist Marjorie Cameron. Apparently, Ryan took a page from his book. That's an important thing to consider about my experiences with Ryan. So much of the time he seemed cryptic, but he wasn't pulling this stuff out of thin air. One needed scholarship to understand what he was getting at.

It's hard to say if the magic worked, but if you look around, it's possible Armageddon already happened. The world is such a mess. It's possible he rode Babalon down that road knowing the apocalypse was in full swing and it was news to the rest of us.

EM

Hamtramck boasted more than fifty bars in its 2.1 square miles, and Chris and I explored most of them. We spent a lot of nights drinking with Ryan as well, but one interesting thing I noticed was that he never became sloppy drunk. He never passed out. Drunken rants, the strange tangential connections of alcohol, but never the stammering imbecilities that plague the drunken mind. Coffee and nicotine were really his narcotics. Even now I recall he smelled of tobacco, usually. I don't think he wore any other scent. No cologne, of course, though he was not above essences, patchoulis, but those didn't define him. It was his stimulants, the tobacco on his clothes, the coffee on his breath that I can recall. But he was curiously not attracted to other stimulants like speed or cocaine. One of the few who knew how to properly intoxicate the mind, in doses. An enviable understanding.

CK

Like me, Ryan preferred women, but his exploratory nature also included men. We shared women and fooled around a few times bisexually, but all this polyamorous debauchery was for a higher tantric purpose. For him, it acted as a ritual. Orgies to raise energy. He treated these sex magic ceremonies with the same intensity as other spiritual endeavors like fasting, renunciation, or yoking desire. His promiscuity was never frivolous. Far from it. Absolute intention was his goal. He never got drunk and woke the next morning regretting what he did.

Relationship boundaries blurred for us as we shared women. Mandy remained his main lover, but others came and went. I couldn't reciprocate his gifts because I was too jealous. My current girlfriend, Olivia Rose, ended up sleeping with him anyway, but I deserved it because I wasn't monogamous either. That was the nature of our circle during that period in Detroit. Perhaps if Olivia Rose and I were more open, and I wasn't so jealous, we could have done things differently. After that, part of me was disappointed in him, and our relationship was never the same.

He had no trouble sharing his partners with others, but his women had an unwritten rule to be faithful. It was a double standard and I pitied his lovers. Magic always came first. Mandy said he often fantasized about her and I having sex without him. We had a threesome on a few occasions and when I asked her why we never did it without him, she said, "He's a polygamist in theory, not in practice. As much as he says he's okay with it, he's not. Not really. He wants to have his cake and eat it too."

It must have been difficult to love him as a woman, knowing you were one of many. I adored him, but not like a woman. More like a son who loves the father, or a student who loves the teacher, or a poet who loves another poet.

But what was happening below the surface when we had these orgies? Was there a magical component I didn't understand? By giving me his women, was that some kind of sacrifice? I'm not sure, but these encounters became the freest sexual experiences in my life, and I look back on them often. A childlike and innocent energy charged them. That seems impossible considering the context. These experiences acted almost like theater, and he became a black sun with us rotating around him. I've had other lovers, both men and women in different polyamorous configurations, but I've never been able to take part in anything of that ilk since, at least not in the same way.

To influence three or four people to engage in his ceremonies showed his power, but the irony is that he didn't need to convince us. He acted according to his own will, and we followed because we knew we could in his presence. He inspired us to be freer and we became voyeurs and exhibitionists acting in his theater.

It would seem that this was all cultish darkness. Far from it. Light and love filled these experiences, but not without a few problems. One time, he had sex with this other woman, Tonya, in front of Mandy and I. Tonya was one of the many women Ryan met at his late-night coffee shops. Mandy believed her to be a temporary diversion in their lives, almost a toy of sorts. Mandy became furious, and she pushed him off. Angrily, Mandy bolted from the room and Ryan ran after her to quell her jealousy. Tonya cried a little, and it was awkward because I barely knew her. Trying to console Tonya, I realized she was in love with Ryan. She played her hand as if she was an easy catch, but her crying made her true feelings obvious. I'm sure this happened with many women and men alike.

After they returned to the room he said, "Io, Pan." *The Thelemic Hymn to Pan* was his way of saying, "I'm sorry, that's your trip, not mine."

EM

Ryan had a way of changing minds by casting things in a new light. He changed my mind about Satan, for instance. I always had conceived of the dark lord as a force of unadulterated evil, in keeping with theological training and common

140

practice. But he made a compelling case for an updated Satan, one best thought of as force rather than pestilence. The teaching hinged on the concept that Satan had been misrepresented. According to Ryan, the notion that Satan was the repository of all the evil of the world was the grossest misrepresentation. A lie of epic proportions that, interestingly, exposed the house of cards that is Western ethics predicated on Christian thought. Satan is, rather, all that is excluded from the light, the cast-off, the Jungian shadow. Embracing him is not a simple pact with God's other, but an understanding of the duality of the universe; a realization, understanding, and consequent acceptance of all that has been cast to the margins of Western society. Satan is all that you've been taught not to think, not to desire, not to feel. And embracing him has the twofold power of not just rejecting a reasonless, constrictive society, but of empowering oneself with all the pent-up energy and force that has been relegated to the basement of the soul.

CK

The affair with Olivia Rose became a huge thorn that escalated into constant fights between Ryan and I. These fights were as mysterious as every other part of our relationship. We didn't voice our differences. Things continued as usual, but pearls of wisdom came less frequently. Aside from sleeping with my girlfriend, other factors pulled us in different directions. He was a notorious hermit. This wasn't the first time he retreated, but I sensed it would be a longer sojourn this time. Was it part of his process? Did we need him to exit so we might understand mutation on our own terms? Was he sick of us? I don't know. I know he faded from our crew as we gained self-reliance, as we gained power, so maybe there's a connection there. We became leaders in our own right, but different from the leaders we may have been in the past. Erik and I were always strong individuals, and we always went against the grain. That was nothing new, but this transformation he guided me through was a different animal. I can only say initiation turned me into a more complete human being who needed his own path, not to follow another path.

Maybe he felt he finished The Work with us. Maybe he needed solitude so he could mutate again. Not sure. But I suspect he did the same thing with his other projects, those people who also struggled with the outcome of their mutations. Perhaps it was a vital step in the transformation to cut the umbilical.

For someone who seemed certain of magic, Ryan carried many insecurities in other areas of life. He remained at odds with most people. As with most eccentrics, he felt conventional people judged him. Paranoia crippled him at times. That was just part of his character. I can understand why. Every time he ventured into public, the indoctrinated individuals outnumbered the broad-minded folk tremendously. A needle in a haystack. This disparity made you feel special at least. He took the time with you because he knew you were ready.

I can see why he wanted to retreat. I witnessed countless occasions where people attacked him for his unorthodox beliefs. He exposed himself too much. People attacked him because of his openness. It was a threat to their bourgeoisie practicality. I saw it time and time again.

He may have felt we didn't need him anymore, and we probably didn't realize at the time what his presence meant to us until he left. That's how most things are in life.

EM

Despite all the time Chris and I spent with Ryan, more and more it felt as though he was growing distant. At first, I wrote it off as just the ebb and flow of any friendship. But it began to become obvious that things were changing. It depressed me a bit. Ryan had meant so much to my intellectual and spiritual growth, and it seemed almost like an admonishment for him to miss a party or an event, or to even not stop by at one in the morning like he was prone to do in the past. Perhaps he was getting less and less from us, and thus felt it best to slowly sever ties. It was always difficult to know for sure the source of his frustration. While he did seem concerned with our recent decisions to become more social, it also felt like he had achieved his goal, and it was now up to us to continue on the path if we so chose.

But an even more depressing possibility laid behind his absence. Ryan would occasionally remind me how fortuitous our meeting had been from the very start. According to him, he went through cycles. Periods when he would retreat deep into himself, and talk to nobody. Stay locked in his room for days. This seemed hard to believe when I first met him, but as I began to see more of the withdrawn side of his personality I understood better what he meant. Had I met him a few years before, or a few later, he might not have even taken the time or energy to accost me, to try and engage on the level I had come to take for granted. It was sad to think of him slowly slipping away, visiting less, speaking less, just fading into the swath of suburbs from which he had sprung. Sad, but then later bittersweet, as I realized that he was right—it was fate, or chance, or just plain luck, that I had encountered him when I had.

CK

The Northeast blackout was an extensive power outage throughout parts of the Midwest and Northeast, and up into Ontario, Canada in 2003. I was working at the Cass Café when it happened around 4pm. At first, people thought it was a normal power outage. After a few hours, people wondered if a terrorist attack happened. 9/11 occurred only two years prior, so people remained on edge.

Everyone at work rejoiced because we closed shop and headed to a friend's house to party with some cocaine and booze. I didn't do blow often, but many other servers and bartenders did it regularly. For a few hours, we partied hard until we realized the power wasn't coming back. Then, we noticed people up and down the street were acting peculiar. Our group talked about the riots and many of us wondered if chaos would once again take hold of the city. Sirens wailed as cop cars zipped back and forth in the distance. We looked at each other for confirmation. It was time to head home.

Dread overtook me as I jumped on my bike and pedaled back to Hamtramck. Still feeling the cocaine, my ride through the New Center and into no-man's-land became more frightening. When I got home, Erik sat there in near darkness. A finality crossed my mind. Was this the end? Candles created an ominous vibe that conquered the place. Was it safe in the flat? The back stairs, our entrance, sported two deadbolts. We eyed the balcony with its lockless door. The rotting balcony needed repair. Nobody would be crazy enough to climb it, would they? We got worried because we kept hearing sirens and an occasional yelling, so we hammered a few nails through the door into the jamb.

We waited out the night scared and ready for looters. Questions ran through my mind. What was the uprising of 1967 like? What would it be like to run down the street as houses burned around me? These thoughts, and the waning cocaine buzz plus the oppressive summer heat, made it hard for me to sleep. All the while, I thought of Ryan and the departure he was making from our lives. Fear had not left me. Was he worried like we were? Probably not. A place like Detroit had different threats than the suburbs, and I suspect Ryan got a kick out of the anarchy.

We made it through the night, but the next day became exceedingly hot. A heat wave settled in and we were dying in our flat without fans. After several hours of this, Olivia Rose called from Boulder, Colorado where she took classes at Naropa. She was worried about us, and said we could go to her parents' and use their pool. We thought it was a lifesaving idea, so we jumped into a battered car Erik had recently bought and headed to the suburbs the back way near Hamtramck Disneyland, a strange outsider art installation near our home. We made it to Mound Road, but the further we drove away from Detroit, the weirder it became. Unlit traffic lights remained common in the city, but in the suburbs they felt alien. On and on we drove like Omega Men, running through four-way stops and barely seeing anybody. A blanket of anxiety and expectation filled my thoughts. Occasionally, we'd see a cop car stroll by, but mostly, the journey remained desolate. During the twenty-minute drive, we saw only a handful of people.

Finally, we arrived at her house. Her sister was there, but she ignored us. We dove into the pool with relish. It felt glorious after a good twenty-four hours without respite from the heat. We swam. The power came back on, so we dried ourselves and joined her sister by the television to see what had happened. CNN stated that it was the world's second most widespread blackout in history, and they were still trying to figure out what happened. The news focused on the terror element. Was it a terror attack? Was it an invasion? The headlines scrolled across the bottom of the screen. For me, it was a strange feeling. Something inside told me America entered a metamorphosis after 9/11. The country headed into the same isolation and darkness I had entered when I came down to the city, that same confrontation with fear, that same unpredictable power that threatened to consume me. The millennium's early years became an initiatory time, not just for me, but also for my country. And like the madness I found in my Cass Corridor apartment, America was losing its mind.

CK

Things began to change. Social interaction became more and more important as I integrated into the scene. Many of these friendships transitioned into love affairs. The sexual experimentation I explored with Ryan pushed me forward. I wanted to see how far I could take it without him, but I was insecure in my strengths. Inertia overtook my life. Some women didn't know about each other. Some were threesomes. Power intoxicated me, and I didn't know how to temper it. I seduced women just to see if I could, but like Bobby Soul, I pushed too far into darkness. Lovers found out about each other. Threesomes became power struggles that destroyed friendships. Word got around. My sexual liberty caused destruction, and people made sure I knew I hurt them. Lots of wreckage followed.

Looking back, I was too inexperienced to understand Ryan's gift, so I abused it. I wasn't ready to take on this much command, and it tore apart those around me. It destroyed me too. It was another important stage of development, but the light and dark sides within his teachings became difficult to reconcile. Bourgeoisie morality was beyond us now. Most of the positions the middle class took were too simple for our expanded outlook. People misconstrued the magnetism, openness, and loving on many levels.

Going around in circles. Partying. Drug experimentation. Sexual conquests. Falling outs. It all became exhausting and my newfound authority turned into a multitude of problems. Ryan's bow-wave wedge became a difficult balance to achieve, and it took many years to hone. My wedge was more of a nine-car pile-up than a clear, strong line, but I learned the lesson.

EM

On a sunny spring day, I was sitting on a bench in the pleasant little square in front of Hamtramck's courthouse. A slight breeze was rattling a chain against the flagpole. Not quite warm enough to take off my jacket, but the snow was starting to melt. I was musing on my time in Detroit, slightly frustrated, but also slightly expectant. I was tired. It was time to move on, and my thoughts were thawing along with the snow.

For all of Ryan's wisdom and fearlessness, he was curiously uninterested in changes of place. He traveled in his car constantly, but rarely left the limits of greater Detroit. Apart from a long weekend we spent together in D.C., he never took trips; living abroad held little interest for him.

In a sense, I admired this attitude. Ryan had his adventures, like the season he spent sleeping in his car while traveling through California, or the time he spent in Alaska working in the hold of a fishing seiner scooping salmon into a huge net that would dangle precariously over his head. And there was northern Michigan—his university days and sweat lodge rituals. Despite, or maybe because of these adventures, he always held that the real space worth exploring was inside. While the outside was beautiful, it was the mere trappings of the true reality hidden within the seeker. While I appreciated his viewpoint, I nevertheless felt a wanderlust. My education seemed incomplete as I thought of all the places I had read about out there for me to discover. As the sun melted the snow and I thought back on the long travails of my time in Detroit, it seemed to me that leaving the city was a necessity if I was to grow further.

CK

After my abuse of power, Ryan's teachings took on a different light. Did I misunderstand the concept of Will, at least in the Thelemic sense? Will wasn't strength, but a point outside morality, separate from it. Like the Taoist concept of *wu wei*, "effortless action" or "non-doing." By approaching people this way, Ryan used Will to align with those who needed help. Or not. To him, the result remained irrelevant either way. He did this without thought of reward. I used my Will to seduce, which is all about reward. I didn't understand the difference. Now, I see it and I've adapted my conduct accordingly. I've become a better person. This was a tough lesson, and I burnt many bridges to learn it.

My connection with Ryan became even more disrupted. He checked out of the parties. He struggled to communicate with people. He showed up less or for a shorter time. Relations became strained between us, and he hung out with a different set of people. He couldn't guide me because he didn't know where I was going. I couldn't learn from him because I had to find the rest on my own.

EM

Something ended in our friend Michael's basement.

It started as most other parties start. Guests took off their coats, pleasantries were exchanged, and between the flow of alcohol and the wafting of smoke, conversations ensued and deepened. But something was in the air. Many of our friends had begun to drift away. Those more spiritually inclined to Boulder and the West Coast, others seeking fame and fortune to New York, and still more exchanging Detroit's winter for the warm sun of New Orleans. The geography of the place heightened the sense of divide. Michael's house, a small 1930s bungalow outside the city in Pontiac, had three levels, splitting partygoers into various floors. Floating from the top to the bottom provided a range of conversations, all intriguing but each with their own hue. I finally found myself in the basement, huddled around an old fireplace Michael had installed. He had left the door open so we could enjoy the flame, and it was a cozy, if dark, place to share conviviality.

And then it happened, an end that I recall vividly. I had stumbled into this fireside discussion mid-stream, but could tell that Ryan was agitated. In fact, I had never seen him angry before, and it struck me that while I felt I knew him as deeply or even deeper than most, my belated arrival to the city meant that my friends knew him more broadly, across his various moods. He was arguing with Chris about the nature and function of rebellion, and how it should be conducted. I gathered that Ryan felt left behind somehow, as if the model of revolt being offered did not include him. The content of the discussion was less important than the underlying dynamics of relationships that were surfacing, and the depth of the rift surprised me. I tried to mitigate, but it was to no avail. A deeper tension was being brought to the surface. Finally, Ryan smashed his glass against the concrete floor and declared, "Well, storm the castle without me!" A tense silence ensued as Ryan's heavy boots tromped upstairs and became lost in the laughter and shouts of the party above.

IV

EM

There was a moment, not so long ago, when I found myself in the midst of a vision. I had been under a lot of strain and felt exhausted. After Detroit, I had moved to Germany for a year on a Fulbright scholarship and from there to Turkey, where I took a job as a professor at a university in Istanbul. But the excitement of life abroad had waned, while my responsibilities to my parents, my wife, and my newborn child had grown. My life was at a crossroads. I had been in Turkey for a decade, and as life there became untenable, it was now time to return home. I sat on a terrace outside my office, gazing into the forest, and beyond that, the Black Sea. I could see a rent open up in the fabric of my life. Everything I had gazed upon over the past ten years appeared new. I felt other to myself, and to the world around me, as if the universe had just tilted ever so slightly so that it now hung at a new angle. The world as I had known it now askew, the possibility for another world opened up—all I had to do was simply walk away, and I could become a new person. Just get up and walk out on the entire scene, shedding history like taking off a coat. Drop all the cares and worries and enter the future clean.

At moments like these I look back at the time I spent with Ryan and gauge my present against my past. I realize that I was trying to get outside—outside of myself, my beliefs, perhaps even time itself—and living in Detroit was about as outside as you could get. There was no telos, no endpoint, no goal. The path was all, and growth was our byword. But from the perspective of middle age, I see now, can only truly see now, how circumscribed we were by our youth. We had the optimism of idealists and believed the future would take care of itself. If we could just keep mutating, there seemed nothing we couldn't achieve. But we left the ends to fend for themselves. It was accumulation we were after, of experience, knowledge, perspective, storing these up against a future where they would be useful. We were constantly striving to make ourselves new, expanding, even if we never thought about what we could grow into. If indeed we cared about becoming anything at all. Now that my future has arrived, and with it, the myriad stresses and strains of a struggling middle age, I ponder retrospectively—did the future take care of itself?

CK

What's he doing now? Over the last ten years, nobody has heard from him. It's perplexing that he severed contact with every person we knew. I can understand why he might not want to talk to me. We had a relationship that was intimate, and often when these kinds of relationships end, it's best to keep a distance. But what about all our mutual friends? Over a dozen people haven't heard from him. Unreturned calls. Connections cut.

Regardless, I saw him one last time. It was about seven years after our falling out. I had five years of Portland behind me and a year abroad in South Korea under my belt. I called him when I returned to Detroit for a visit. I'm surprised he agreed to meet me. I met him at his new place in the suburbs, a mere few miles from his previous apartment. Somehow, he secured a huge house. This seemed odd, especially considering his job probably didn't pay well. He worked as a caretaker for a mentally challenged boy.

In the past, he always lived in small, cookie-cutter apartments. But this house proved the opposite; it stood majestic, a three-story building from the 1920s. I entered the building and felt a strong sense of the paranormal. What he did in the house was anyone's guess, but the place felt foreboding, deep with harrowing energy. I took off my winter boots and coat. He motioned me in. I turned from the door into the foyer. A stained-glass window glittered in the hall that screamed sacred geometry. He acknowledged it by saying, "That's why I got the place."

Cryptic as always.

The house was empty, with a minimal amount of furniture with entire rooms vacant. The building's immensity screamed excess, but the lack of furnishings made it utilitarian. He showed me around, taking me from space to space. Last, he showed me where he performed his rituals: his ceremonial area in the enormous attic.

Once again, the man had his contradictions.

The conversation was brief, but I was happy to see him. He seemed a little uncomfortable when I spoke of my time overseas so I kept that short. We talked a little about the occult studies I completed in Portland. We chatted about the Holy Guardian Angel because I found mine in Portland and he became excited about my findings. He told me he was seeing a new woman but he never mentioned her name. And then that was it. He became silent, and I knew it was time to leave. The entire visit lasted less than an hour.

I left the place and as I walked into the snow, I knew it was the last time I'd see him. I looked back, but he had already shut the door. I stared at the house and it seemed like a prison. How often did he leave it? Did he have any friends these days? The whole scene reminded me of the

House of Usher. I assumed that he must have found a new circle, but something told me this wasn't the case, and I also wondered if there was an actual girlfriend. Someone like him should influence people, be out there searching, but part of me knew he hadn't done that. The hermit went too deep this time.

I couldn't surrender my curiosity about what his life must be like. Was he all right? How far had he evolved since our Detroit and Hamtramck days? How deep into magic had he delved? Perhaps so deep he couldn't even identify with people anymore. The thought saddened me. All I could see for him was a lingering in this gothic isolation.

Thinking of this time makes me consider how far I've come. Detroit and its excesses are far behind me. I still dabble around a little with psychedelics and alcohol, but I satiated that relentless push toward oblivion. I've done my share of turning people on like he did, like he said we should back then. But why should I bother if the destination is a lonely hermitage? Regardless, I identify with his plight. It's been difficult for me to be social. My journeys abroad have created long stretches of loneliness. While traveling, eccentrics seek that energy in me, just like they did in him. Now, I see how this can exhaust a person. Once a mystic understands that the seeker needs that metamorphosis, the mystic knows it will drain their energy. At first this seems welcome because you're doing The Work. But after a few experiences, it feels like vampirism—that lost, needy look of a person who's trying to cling to a life raft, and the mystic appears at the right time, another synchronicity to make one believe one's on the right track. These days, I dread these moments because they're messy and they cause pain. I relent to these situations but not without protest. I understand why he shut himself away.

EM

Ryan provided a glimpse of possibility. The power of nega-tion, the ability to quit, to say "no" to the world that was bequeathed him, the power to be alone, to be able to be alone, were his. To step outside yourself to take a fresh glimpse. Though of course he didn't escape forever. If it seemed so to us, it was probably due to our naiveté, and the novelty of even seeing it at all. He needed solitude, but one of the ironies of his life was that he was seldom alone. His independence attracted so many others, also desperate to escape. In him they saw a catalyst, someone to push them beyond themselves. He was, in many ways, a drug, but one that could only be replenished in isolation. But the flash second of seeing someone get outside the trappings of the world was enough. It was a chance, a clearing in the woods where one could get their bearings. In this flash second when it all made sense it didn't matter anyway. Then there was neither time nor space, nor anything but you and him and everything and nothing. And we shared many such moments, many such.

CK

Enter the ruins. Strip down. Get burned at the stake and rise like the Phoenix. That was his view of my journey downtown, a mythical exodus into a ruined city to die a psychological death. Envious of my metamorphosis, he would often grill me about what I was going through. What were my chal-lenges? What was it for?

I often asked him, "Why don't you move down here? Wouldn't facing similar challenges make you grow too?"

He replied, "Marquette was my ruins. The man who put the gun to my head was my trial by fire. A Native American sweat lodge was my crucible. Magic always remains the fuel."

He would say, "Detach from the past. Cut the tether."

I did just that, and I continue to do so. That's how I honor him. I live for a time, I dig deep and learn, and then I depart. I return to see how far I've come, to gauge my progress, to understand another mutation. I run, but the lessons find me. It's all a self-assessment to see if I'm still on the path. Fleeing to a new country, a new job, a new relationship, all these things test whether I avoid stagnation, whether I keep balance, a place he referred to as the Pleroma—to follow my Will, to blossom into an engaged person, to dig deeper. Blast down the geographic, economic, and sociological walls that society builds to contain me. Break down the self-imposed limits, tear down histories, confront emotions, challenge myself.

His teachings showed me that an engaged individual must become a psychic spelunker. It's essential. Dive deep into mind. Spend time alone. Living in a culture that doesn't speak English makes this easy to do. I almost always feel alone even when I'm with people from my country. And maybe that's the real transformation I went through. The mutation made me separate.

EM

Now in my wistful glances backward, I wonder where he is today. I have not seen him in over a decade. Has he outpaced us? In terms of his physical movement, I doubt it. He was a mutation cast forth from the Detroit suburbs, and he probably resides within the same 50-mile radius of his birth. Chris and I have traveled across the world in opposite directions, residing in multiple cultures far different than America. But he still remains the gauge by which we measure our spiritual growth. He is the standard. Did we outpace him? Most probably not. His mutations were compulsive, unavoidable, part of his very self. Mine feel halting, stuttering, and uncertain. I stumble forward, groping for a way out of the dark. He strides. But then again, with regards to spiritual development, one never knows. The greatest shifts often come after the longest stasis.

CK

Am I still on the path?

I think so. I feel like it.

Often, I come into contact with people from different places and walks of life. Their reactions remain the same. They say, "Where you from?" I say, "Detroit." They give me a look of pity, like "Oh... I'm sorry." I roll my eyes. Every Detroiter will tell you how proud they are to proclaim the city as home. It's a badge. It's an honor. I did it. I survived. I'm not dead. I gleaned the pearl from the experience. I won the treasure. That's what we say.

But am I still on the mission?

Yes, but it's a secret mission, a surreptitious war that people don't know we need to fight.

Ryan knew this. For him, mutation was a crusade, a mission to save freethinkers from the corporate industrial complex through consciousness expansion. He said the informed person (the magician) should inform the seeker (the neophyte) and reveal truth if possible. Person by person, this should happen in a grassroots manner like it has for millennia.

He didn't want to be a martyr, hence the secrecy. Ryan remained invisible and liked it that way. By writing this book we've exposed him but for good cause I believe. We've heaped so much love upon him and also illustrated both his and our weaknesses, but the one thing to remember is that he wouldn't have influenced us if we hadn't been in the position to accept it. This says as much about him as it does us, and where we were at that time.

I haven't seen the man in almost ten years, but I suspect if he walked through the door, the conversation might start back at that sweet spot. All the great and terrible events shared in our long friendship might fade into the background. Our betrayals might disappear. It's rare to find that energy, and when it's gone, it's a large hole to fill. If I ever said this, he'd shrug and say, "You got your own battery, man. Always have, always will."

EM

So I call out to him as if calling to my past, so desirable yet tantalizingly just beyond reach. Bygone days not at all carefree, but still open, filled with possibility, pregnant. My life has given birth to joy, but also to care, remorse, frustration, and longing. Oh, to be on a train platform, waiting with a ticket in hand. But I'm on a train pulling into the station. I'm a weary passenger, disembarking, wondering what I'll eat tonight, where I'll sleep, how I'll make out. He freed me from many of my cages, not just with his ideas, but with his own careful attention. And his love. He also helped me to develop a set of picklocks for subsequent cages and traps I've found myself in over the years. For all that I'm extremely thankful. But the path is uncertain, and one never knows what lies ahead. And that uncertainty is both a blessing and a curse, the fraught place where I struggle to understand how to live.

CK

One last memory to relate.

Back in the Cass Corridor days, Ryan co-opted my copy of Gandhi's autobiography. I could never tell if he was being ironic about his interest in the man or perhaps he was just saving me from that road, saving me from myself.

Ryan wasn't a fan of enlightenment. Not the way people usually see it. It wasn't a goal to him. He didn't buy the "gurus and their sheep" (his words). That's why he was so convincing. His discernment tore that shit to shreds. His honesty made that impossible. He could see right through it. That was his mission, to invalidate these jokers, to invalidate their illusions. He was the spiritual flashlight shining into the dark.

As I get older, life gets more complicated and many of life's illusions become difficult to navigate. A little dose of truth and one can't go back. Then, these truths mutate too and one realizes it's all a big mystery and the questions become answerless. When I was in my 20s it all seemed simple. Read books. Make love. Produce art. Live adventures. Try to have a soul while you do it.

These days, I'm not so sure.

If one can attain enlightenment, then one can also lose it. Ryan's view differs from this because it's a trajectory without direction, movement without a goal, a process. True freedom.

Once at a party, I got entangled in a conversation where some people claimed enlightenment. I asked, "How do you know you're enlightened?" Answers included: "I read a book that changed my life" or "I had an experience that woke me up."

I replied, "So, it's all over? You reached it? You found the answer?"

The people nodded their heads, and I said, "Then, I don't think you're enlightened."

They looked annoyed. They didn't agree with my opinion and it seemed like I insulted them by diminishing their achievement. After a moment of letting it sink in, I added, "Can't the mystery satisfy you, the unraveling?"

They looked at me like I was crazy. How could anyone be satisfied with unknowing? But that's the most important point in all we've written. Ryan wanted you to transcend the names and words. As he was fond of saying, "True myth is a means of experiencing a mystery. A true mystery can only be directly experienced. It is itself, plain and simple." He wanted you to become the mystery. He wanted you to be the myth.

Regardless, the most priceless lesson I learned from Ryan was The Work never stops. Like evolution, it should always roll on and it's your job to be the natural selector, to keep asking the questions but to know you may never find answers. Enlightenment becomes a trap because it means you've stopped growing. You reached a goal. What goal? Did you discover that you're one with the universe? Big deal. People have done that forever. Animals already know this. Now what? How do you use it? How do you refine? How do you transcend it?

At the time I knew him, I was so inexperienced. I didn't understand this and I regret we never explored this idea together. Now, I'm most content feeling that the mysteries are wondrous, and I enjoy the notion I can't solve them. I like that big "Why?"

If he was here, he'd just snicker at our existential struggles, shrug his shoulders, and say, "I don't know what to tell you."

Acknowledgments

The authors would like to warmly thank Julie Doxsee, Jeffrey Kars, Andrew Leigh, Jessica Leigh, Abigail Mallin, Erik Marshall, and Stacy Muszynski for their helpful and supportive comments on the various drafts of this manuscript. Any errors, of course, remain our own.

We would also like to thank Director and Publisher of Cornerstone Press, Ross Tangedal, for his unflagging support throughout the publication process. The book would have been impossible without him. Brett Hill, Editorial Director, provided helpful comments as well as enthusiasm for the manuscript, and we relished both. Thanks also goes out to Managing Editor Kirsten Faulkner for helping keep us on track, as well as to Julia Kaufman who worked on the cover design. We would like to heartily thank everyone at Cornerstone Press who helped contribute to the book. It was a joy to work with such a wonderful team, and we certainly could not have done it without each of you.

Erik Mortenson would like to thank Lia McCoskey for her support throughout the writing, editing, and publishing process. And last but certainly not least, Erik wants to thank his daughter, Zelda. Her warmth, curiosity and love are a constant inspiration, not only for this project, but for life in general.

ERIK MORTENSON is a literary scholar, writer, translator, and faculty member in English at Lake Michigan College in Benton Harbor, Michigan. After earning a PhD from Wayne State University in Detroit, Erik spent a year as a Fulbright Lecturer in Germany before journeying to Koç University in Istanbul to help found the English and Comparative Literature Department. After spending more than a decade abroad, he returned to the U.S. shortly after the 2016 coup. His scholarly work focuses on American literary and visual texts and their intersection with the cultural concerns of the twentieth-century. Erik has published numerous journal articles and book chapters, as well as three books: *Capturing the Beat Moment: Cultural Politics and the Poetics of Presence* (2011), *Ambiguous Borderlands: Shadow Imagery in Cold War American Culture* (2016), and *Translating the Counterculture: The Reception of the Beats in Turkey* (2018).

CHRISTOPHER KRAMER (Christopher of Detroit) is the author of the novels *The Invisible Histories of the Spiral Mountain* (2014), *The Erotic Tales of Bucephalus* (2017), and *Dominique's Confession: A Roaring Twenties Dark Romance* (2020). In his tales of magic and mysticism, he examines philosophical dualities, transitions of the psyche, alternate realities, and spiritual revelations. Christopher is also an artist and illustrator with over twenty exhibitions. His illustrations appear in the *Tenebre Horror Anthology* (2021) and *Illustrated Worlds* magazine (2023). His work also appears in the first edition of *Dark Spirits: The Magical Art of Rosaleen Norton and Austin Osman Spare* (2012) in a limited-edition print.